family circle®

Modern Australian food

The Family Circle® Promise of Success

Welcome to the world of Confident Cooking, created for you in the Australian **Family Circle® Test Kitchen,** where recipes are double-tested by our team of home economists to achieve a high standard of success—and delicious results every time.

MURDOCH BOOKS®
Sydney • London • Vancouver • New York

All recipes are double-tested by our team of home economists. When we test our recipes, we rate them for ease of preparation. The following cookery ratings are on the recipes in this book, making them easy to use and understand.

A single Cooking with Confidence symbol indicates a recipe that is simple and generally quick to make—perfect for beginners.

Two symbols indicate the need for just a little more care and a little more time.

Three symbols indicate special dishes that need more investment in time, care and patience—but the results are worth it.

TEST KITCHEN PERFECTION

You'll never make a wrong move with a Family Circle step-by-step cookbook. Our team of home economists has tested and refined the recipes so that you can create fabulous food in your own kitchen. Follow our easy instructions and step-by-step photographs and you'll feel like there is a master chef in the kitchen guiding you every step of the way.

IMPORTANT

Those who might be at risk from the effects of salmonella food poisoning (the elderly, pregnant women, young children and those suffering from immune deficiency diseases) should consult their GP with any concerns about eating raw eggs.

The Publisher thanks the following for their assistance: MUD Australia, Chief Australia, Breville Holdings Pty Ltd, Kambrook, Sheldon & Hammond, Bertolli Olive Oil; Southcorp Appliances.

Front cover: *Tempura prawns with soba noodles and dashi broth (page 38).*
Inside front cover: *Oysters with four toppings (page 25).*
Back cover: *Frozen zabaglione with Marsala sauce (page 96).*

CONTENTS

Top: *Beef fillet with roasted tomato Béarnaise (page 58).* **Bottom:** *Steamed lemon grass and ginger chicken with Asian greens (page 45), Berry ricotta cream tartlets (page 89).*

The best produce

Good food demands great produce: using good-quality ingredients will ensure maximum flavour and texture. Whatever their country of origin, most of these items are now readily available either at the supermarket or in greengrocers or delicatessens. Buy the best you can afford and taste the results.

Asian greens (from left to right)
Chinese broccoli is traditionally known as gai larn. It has slightly leathery leaves and thick, green stems—both are used in cooking. *Baby bok choy* A mild vegetable related to Chinese cabbage. It is great stir-fried, braised or steamed and needs very little cooking. *Choy sum* is otherwise known as flowering cabbage and often has yellow flowers. The stems and leaves are eaten.

Bird's-eye chilli: A very hot, small red or green chilli about 1–3 cm long. They can be bought fresh, dried or pickled in brine, but fresh is best.

Chinese roast duck and pork: Chinese roast duck is a crisp, dark, glossy-skinned duck that can be bought ready to eat from Asian barbecue food shops or restaurants. The pork, or char siu, is coated in a thick sweet glaze before cooking and can be eaten cold or heated and added to other dishes.

Couscous: This is a granular semolina. A favourite in North African cuisine, use it as a base for flavours. Instant couscous, the most common variety, cooks very quickly.

Extra virgin olive oil: Essentially the same as virgin olive oil, but with very low acidity, it comes from the first pressing of olives. It is not really suitable for cooking as the flavour is lost when heated but it is great with pasta or in salad dressings.

Fish sauce: This seasoning is popular in Southeast Asian cuisine. Made by extracting the liquid from salted, fermented fish, it is a clear brown liquid with a pungent salty flavour. Use it sparingly as the flavour is very strong.

Kaffir lime leaves: The dark green, aromatic leaves from the kaffir lime tree have an incomparable flavour and perfume. They are available fresh, frozen or dried—the fresh leaves have an especially intense flavour. Each leaf has a figure of eight shape, and is usually broken in half before use. In our recipes, we have treated one half of the figure of eight as one leaf.

Lemon grass: A thick-stemmed herb with pale green–grey leaves, lemon grass has a lemony flavour and aroma and is an important ingredient in Thai cuisine. The thicker, paler part of the stem is most commonly used. Dried lemon grass is available but it has an inferior flavour.

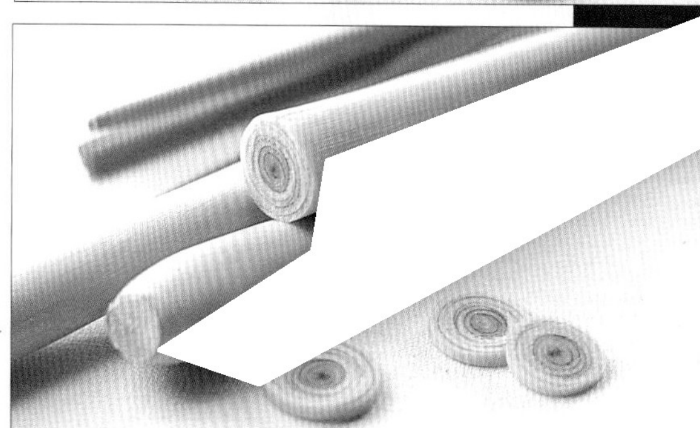

Mirin and sake: Mirin is a low-alcohol, sweet Japanese cooking wine made from glutinous rice, which is used as a sweetener for savoury Japanese cuisine. Cooking sake is very similar, but without the sweetness of mirin. A more refined version of sake is a popular drink in Japan. Mirin and sake are available in Asian supermarkets and Japanese speciality stores.

Mushrooms *(clockwise from front left)*

Oyster mushrooms are a fan or oyster-shell shaped mushroom, pale creamy grey or brown in colour with a slightly peppery flavour that becomes milder when cooked.

Shiitake mushrooms are originally from Japan and Korea. These strongly aromatic and meaty flavoured mushrooms are available either fresh or dried—dried ones need to be reconstituted in hot water before use and have a stronger flavour. The stems are tough and must be discarded, but can be used to flavour stocks.

Shimeji are a delicate-flavoured Japanese mushroom, pale grey–brown and grown in clumps. They have a slightly concave cap on a long stem.

Enoki are a delicate, pale cream or white mushroom with long stems and very small caps. They have a mild yeasty or fruity flavour and can be eaten raw or cooked. Use as fresh as possible.

Palm sugar: Also known as jaggery, palm sugar is popular in Southeast Asian foods. It is an unrefined sugar sold in blocks or jars and ranges in colour from pale gold to dark brown. It is a richly flavoured, aromatic sugar extracted from the sap of various palm trees. Soft brown sugar can be substituted.

Polenta: These coarsely or finely ground dried grains of corn are used in savoury and sweet dishes. Polenta can be served either soft or firm, depending on the coarseness of the grain and the amount of liquid used. Instant polenta takes only a few minutes to cook. (Also known as cornmeal.)

Preserved lemons: Lemons are preserved in salt for about 30 days and develop a soft texture and a distinctive, pungent flavour. They are popular in Moroccan cookery, but should be used sparingly. Rinse well and remove the white pith and flesh before using.

Puy lentils: A small, slate green pulse from France. Reputed to have the best flavour and texture of all lentils, they are only available dried. Buy them in gourmet food stores or delicatessens. They are eaten as a side dish or as a base for savoury meals.

Red Asian shallots: Small purplish red onions with a concentrated flavour, commonly used in Asian cookery. They grow in bulbs and are sold in segments that look like large cloves of garlic. If necessary, you can substitute one small red onion for 3–4 red Asian shallot segments.

Saffron threads: These reddish–orange threads are the stigmas of the crocus flower. Saffron is the most expensive spice in the world, but only a small amount is needed to give a vivid colour and a subtle flavour. The strands are generally infused in a little hot water before using.

Sea salt flakes: These flakes come from the evaporation of sea water. Sea salt flakes have a clean flavour perfect for the table or in cooking.

Vanilla bean: A long, thin pod that is the fruit of a large orchid. Highly aromatic, it has a rich, smooth flavour that is often infused into desserts. The seeds from the pod can also be scraped into liquid for extra flavour and a speckled appearance.

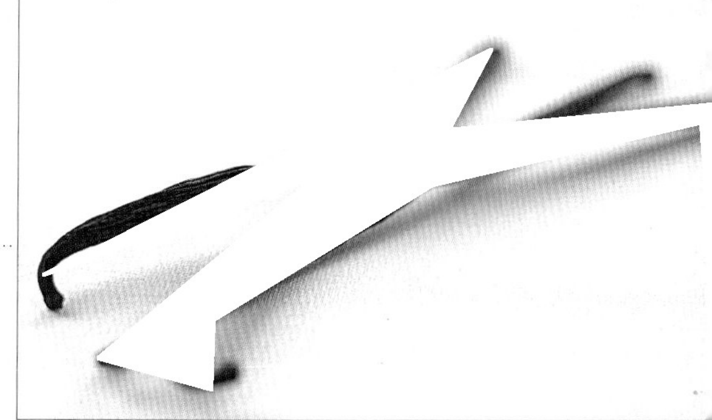

Items that are not available at the supermarket are available in specialist shops.

ENTREES & MAINS

CORN AND LEMON GRASS SOUP WITH YABBIES

Preparation time: 30 minutes
Total cooking time: 1 hour 50 minutes
Serves 4 (6 as an entrée)

4 corn cobs
1 tablespoon oil
1 leek (white part only), chopped
1 celery stick, chopped
3 stems lemon grass (white part only), bruised
2 cloves garlic, crushed
1 teaspoon ground cumin
1 teaspoon ground coriander
3/4 teaspoon ground white pepper
3 kaffir lime leaves
3 cups (750 ml) chicken stock
800 ml coconut milk
1/2 cup (125 ml) cream
2 teaspoons butter
3 cloves garlic, crushed, extra
1/2 teaspoon sambal oelek
1.2 kg cooked yabbies or crayfish, peeled and shredded
1 tablespoon finely chopped fresh coriander leaves

1 Trim the kernels from the corn. Heat the oil in a large saucepan over medium heat, add the leek, celery and lemon grass and stir for 10 minutes, or until the leek is soft. Add the garlic, cumin, coriander and 1/2 teaspoon of the pepper and cook, stirring, for 1–2 minutes, or until fragrant. Add the corn, lime leaves, stock and coconut milk, stir well and simmer, stirring occasionally, for 1 1/2 hours. Remove from the heat and cool slightly.
2 Remove the lemon grass and lime leaves and blend the mixture in batches in a food processor until smooth.
3 Push the mixture through a sieve with a wooden spoon. Repeat.
4 Return to a large clean saucepan, add the cream, and warm gently.
5 Melt the butter in a small frying pan over medium heat, add the extra garlic, sambal oelek, remaining pepper and a pinch of salt and stir for 1 minute. Add the yabby meat, stir for a further minute, or until heated through, then remove from the heat and stir in the fresh coriander.
6 Ladle the soup into shallow soup bowls, then place a mound of yabby meat in the centre of each bowl. Serve.

NUTRITION PER SERVE (4)
Protein 15 g; Fat 60 g; Carbohydrate 25 g; Dietary Fibre 7 g; Cholesterol 105 mg; 2957 kJ (705 cal)

Using a sharp knife, cut the corn kernels off the cob.

Push all the liquid through a sieve with a wooden spoon.

ROASTED DUCK PIZZA

Preparation time: 30 minutes + 45 minutes standing
Total cooking time: 25 minutes
Serves 2 (4 as an entrée)

- 7 g sachet dried yeast
- 1 teaspoon sugar
- 1/2 teaspoon ground coriander
- 1/2 teaspoon five-spice powder
- 2 cups (250 g) plain flour
- 1/4 cup (60 ml) hoisin sauce
- 1 small red capsicum, cut into thin strips
- 1/2 Chinese roasted duck, flesh cut into strips
- 1 cup (125 g) grated Cheddar
- 1/2 cup (60 g) sliced spring onions
- fresh coriander, to serve

1 To make the pizza base, pour 2/3 cup (170 ml) warm water into a large bowl and sprinkle on the yeast, sugar, spices and 1/2 teaspoon salt. Mix well. Leave in a warm draught-free area for 15 minutes, or until foamy.
2 Add half the flour to the bowl, mix, then add the rest. Knead for 15 minutes, or until smooth, adding 1 tablespoon water if the dough is too dry. Shape into a ball, then put in a lightly oiled bowl, cover with a tea towel and leave in a warm place for 30 minutes, or until the dough has doubled in size.
3 Preheat the oven to moderate 180°C (350°F/Gas 4). Knead the dough gently for 1 minute, then divide in two. Roll out half the dough, then gently press into a 28 cm pizza tray with oiled fingers. Freeze the rest.
4 Spread the hoisin sauce over the prepared pizza base, leaving a 2 cm border. Sprinkle with the capsicum, duck and cheese.
5 Bake for 20–25 minutes, or until the dough is cooked and the topping is golden. Sprinkle with spring onion and coriander, then serve.

NUTRITION PER SERVE (2)
Protein 94 g; Fat 44 g; Carbohydrate 108 g; Dietary Fibre 10 g; Cholesterol 414 mg; 5218 kJ (1246 cal)

Leave the yeast mixture in a draught-free place until foamy.

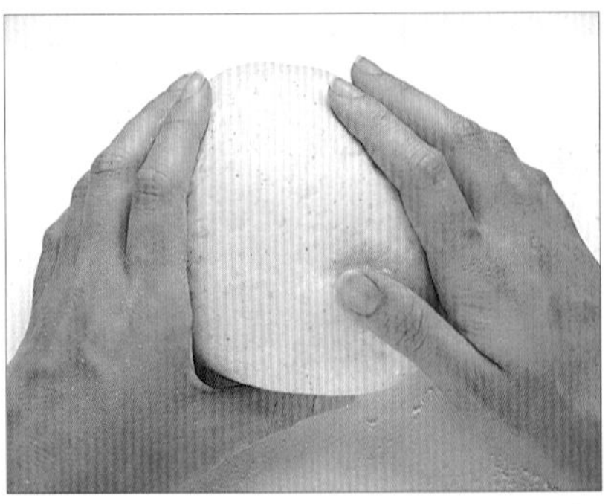

Knead the dough until it is smooth, then shape into a ball.

With oiled fingers, gently press half the dough into a pizza tray.

ASIAN MUSHROOM RISOTTO

Preparation time: 20 minutes + 20 minutes soaking
Total cooking time: 45 minutes
Serves 4 (6 as an entrée)

10 g dried Chinese mushrooms
2 cups (500 ml) vegetable stock
2 tablespoons soy sauce
1/3 cup (80 ml) mirin
150 g Swiss brown mushrooms
150 g oyster mushrooms
100 g fresh shiitake mushrooms
150 g shimeji mushrooms
2 tablespoons butter
1 tablespoon olive oil
1 onion, finely chopped
3 cloves garlic, crushed
1 tablespoon finely chopped fresh ginger
2 cups (440 g) arborio rice
100 g enoki mushrooms, trimmed
2 tablespoons snipped fresh chives
shaved Parmesan, to garnish (optional)

1 Put the Chinese mushrooms in a bowl, cover with 2 1/2 cups (625 ml) hot water and soak for 20 minutes, then drain, reserving the liquid. Remove the stems and thinly slice the caps.

2 Heat the vegetable stock, soy sauce, mirin, reserved mushroom liquid and 1 cup (250 ml) water in a large saucepan, bring to the boil, then reduce the heat and keep at a low simmer, skimming off any scum that forms on the surface.

3 Trim and slice the Swiss brown, oyster and shiitake mushrooms, discarding any woody ends. Trim the shimeji and pull apart into small clumps. Melt 1 tablespoon of the butter in a large saucepan over medium heat, add all the mushrooms except the Chinese and enoki and cook, stirring, for 3 minutes, or until wilted, then remove from the pan.

4 Heat the oil and remaining butter in the same saucepan over medium heat, add the chopped onion and cook, stirring, for 4–5 minutes, or until the onion is soft and just starting to brown. Add the garlic and ginger and stir well until fragrant. Add the rice and stir for 1 minute, or until it is well coated in the oil mixture.

5 Gradually add 1/2 cup (125 ml) of the hot stock to the rice. Stir constantly over medium heat until nearly all the liquid has been absorbed. Continue adding more stock, 1/2 cup (125 ml) at a time, stirring constantly for 20–25 minutes, or until all of the stock has been absorbed and the rice is tender.

6 Add all the mushrooms and stir well. Season to taste with salt and cracked black pepper. Garnish with the chives and shaved Parmesan and serve immediately.

NUTRITION PER SERVE (4)
Protein 17 g; Fat 15 g; Carbohydrate 92 g; Dietary Fibre 8 g; Cholesterol 28 mg; 2397 kJ (573 cal)

Divide the shimeji and slice the Swiss brown, oyster and shiitake mushrooms.

Stir constantly until nearly all the liquid has been absorbed.

CAULIFLOWER SOUP WITH SMOKED SALMON CROUTONS

Preparation time: 25 minutes
Total cooking time: 35 minutes
Serves 4 as an entrée

Croutons
1 loaf day-old white bread, sliced lengthways (see Note)
2 tablespoons butter, melted
1 clove garlic, crushed
150 g smoked salmon or gravlax
1 tablespoon finely chopped fresh dill

Soup
1 tablespoon oil
1 leek (white part only), chopped
1 clove garlic, chopped, extra
400 g cauliflower, cut into florets
1 potato, chopped
1 cup (250 ml) chicken stock
1 cup (250 ml) milk
1 1/4 cups (315 ml) cream
1 tablespoon horseradish cream
1 tablespoon lemon juice
1 tablespoon snipped fresh chives

1 To make the croutons, preheat the oven to slow 150°C (300°F/Gas 2). Brush three slices of the bread on both sides with the combined butter and garlic, then season with salt. Cut off the crusts, cut each slice into four long strips, then carefully transfer the strips to a baking tray, spacing them a little apart. Bake for 30 minutes, or until crisp and golden.
2 Meanwhile, heat the oil in a large saucepan, add the leek and extra garlic and cook over medium heat for 6–8 minutes, or until the leek is soft but not brown. Increase the heat to high, add the cauliflower, potato, stock and milk and bring just to the boil. Reduce the heat and simmer, covered, for 20 minutes, or until the potato and cauliflower have softened.
3 Cool the mixture slightly, then transfer to a blender or food processor and purée until smooth. Return to a clean saucepan and add the cream, horseradish and lemon. Reheat gently for 5 minutes, then add the chives.
4 Cut the salmon into strips the same width as the croutons and lay along the top of each crouton. Sprinkle with the dill. Serve the soup in deep bowls with two long croutons for each person.

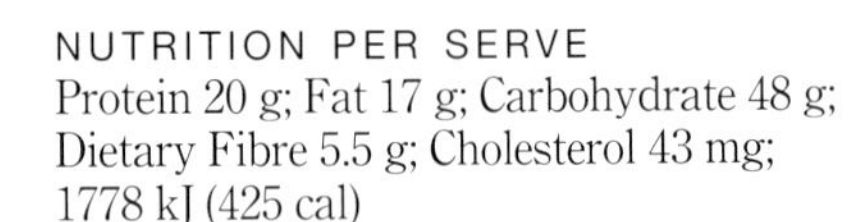

NUTRITION PER SERVE
Protein 20 g; Fat 17 g; Carbohydrate 48 g; Dietary Fibre 5.5 g; Cholesterol 43 mg; 1778 kJ (425 cal)

COOK'S FILE

NOTE: Buy an unsliced loaf and slice it yourself or ask your baker to do it.

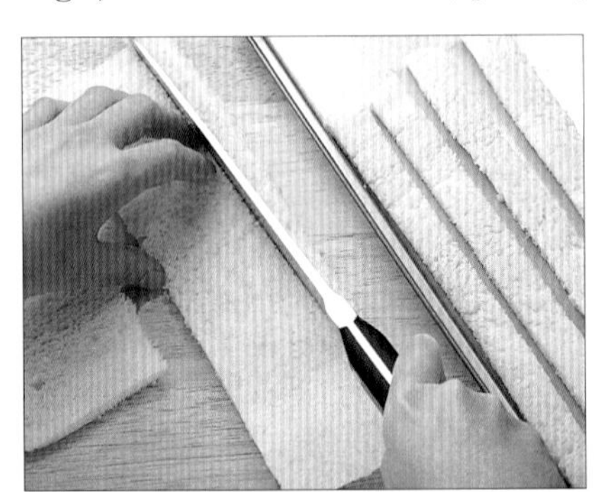

Cut the bread slices into four long strips, then place on a baking tray.

Blend the cooled cauliflower mixture until it is smooth.

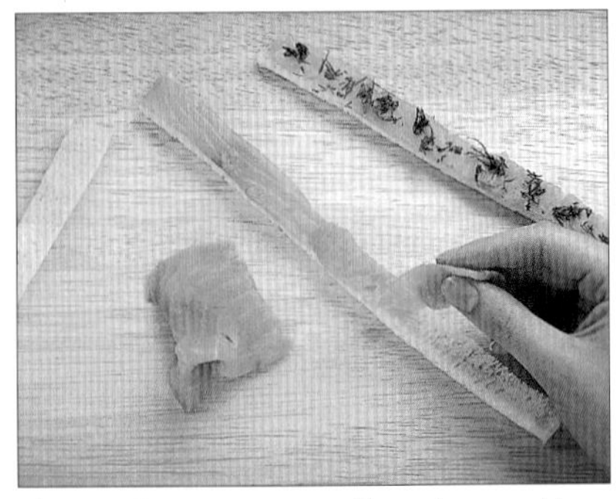

Cover the croutons with salmon strips, then sprinkle with dill.

DEEP-FRIED CALAMARI IN CHICKPEA BATTER WITH PARSLEY SALAD

Preparation time: 15 minutes + 30 minutes standing
Total cooking time: 10 minutes
Serves 4 as an entrée

Deep-fried calamari
150 g besan (chickpea flour)
1 1/2 teaspoons bittersweet smoked paprika or normal paprika
1 1/2 teaspoons ground cumin
1/2 teaspoon baking powder
1 cup (250 ml) soda water
oil, for deep-frying
6 calamari, cleaned and sliced into rings about 8 mm wide

Parsley salad
1/4 preserved lemon, rinsed, pith and flesh removed
1/4 cup (60 ml) lemon juice
1/4 cup (60 ml) extra virgin olive oil
1 clove garlic, finely chopped
1 cup (20 g) fresh flat-leaf parsley
harissa, to serve (optional)

1 To make the batter, sift the besan, paprika, cumin and baking powder into a bowl, add 1/4 teaspoon pepper, mix together and make a well in the centre. Gradually add the soda water, whisking until smooth. Season with salt. Cover, then leave for 30 minutes.
2 Cut the lemon rind into very thin slivers. To make the dressing, whisk the lemon juice, extra virgin olive oil and garlic together in a bowl.
3 Fill a large heavy-based saucepan or wok one third full of oil and heat until a cube of bread dropped into the oil browns in 15 seconds.
4 Dip the calamari into the batter, allowing any excess to drip away. Cook in batches for 30–60 seconds, or until pale gold and crisp all over. Drain well on crumpled paper towels and keep warm.
5 Add the parsley and lemon slivers to the dressing, tossing to coat the leaves. Divide the leaves among four bowls or plates. Top with the calamari rings and serve with harissa.

NUTRITION PER SERVE
Protein 14 g; Fat 27 g; Carbohydrate 14 g; Dietary Fibre 5 g; Cholesterol 90 mg; 1470 kJ (350 cal)

Whisk the batter ingredients together until smooth.

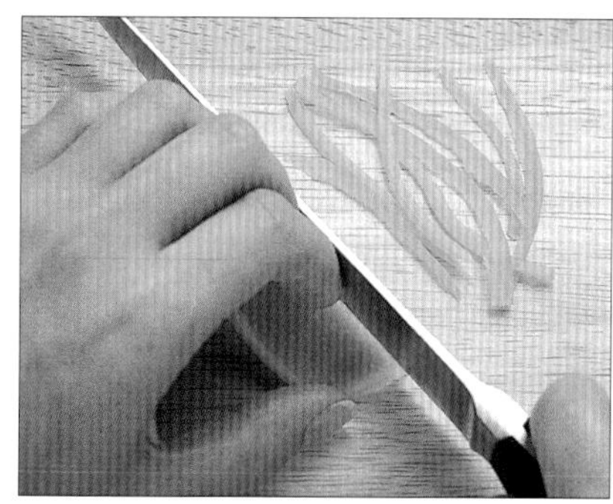

Using a sharp knife, cut the lemon rind into very thin slivers.

EGGPLANT, CAPSICUM, PESTO AND GOAT'S MILK CHEESE STACK

Preparation time: 20 minutes + 30 minutes standing
Total cooking time: 15 minutes
Serves 4 as an entrée

1 kg eggplant, cut into twelve 1.5 cm slices (ends discarded)
1 large red capsicum
olive oil, for pan-frying
1 cup (45 g) rocket leaves
100 g goat's milk cheese
shredded rocket or basil, to garnish
balsamic vinegar, to serve (optional)
olive oil, to serve (optional)

Pesto
1 1/2 cups (75 g) firmly packed fresh basil
2 cloves garlic
2 tablespoons pine nuts, toasted
1 tablespoon lemon juice
1 1/2 tablespoons grated Parmesan
1/2 cup (125 ml) olive oil

1 Rub salt generously into the eggplant slices, then sit in a colander for 30 minutes. Rinse under cold water and pat the eggplant dry.
2 Cut the capsicum into large pieces, removing the seeds and membrane. Place, skin-side-up, under a hot grill until the skin blackens and blisters. Cool in a plastic bag, then peel away the skin. Slice thinly.
3 To make the pesto, combine the basil, garlic, pine nuts, lemon juice and Parmesan in a food processor or blender and process until finely minced. With the motor running, slowly pour in the oil and blend until smooth.
4 Lightly cover the base of a frying pan with oil and heat over medium heat. Add the eggplant in batches and cook both sides until golden, adding more oil as needed. Drain on crumpled paper towels and keep warm.
5 To assemble, lay a few rocket leaves on a plate. Place one slice of eggplant on the rocket, then top with some more rocket leaves, a heaped teaspoon of pesto, one eighth of the capsicum and one eighth of the goat's milk cheese. Repeat, making two layers and finish with a final slice of eggplant. Dollop some pesto on the top of the stack, sprinkle with shredded rocket or basil and season with pepper. Repeat, making three more stacks. Drizzle balsamic vinegar and olive oil around the plate, if desired. Serve immediately.

NUTRITION PER SERVE
Protein 12 g; Fat 55 g; Carbohydrate 8.5 g; Dietary Fibre 7 g; Cholesterol 24 mg; 2397 kJ (573 cal)

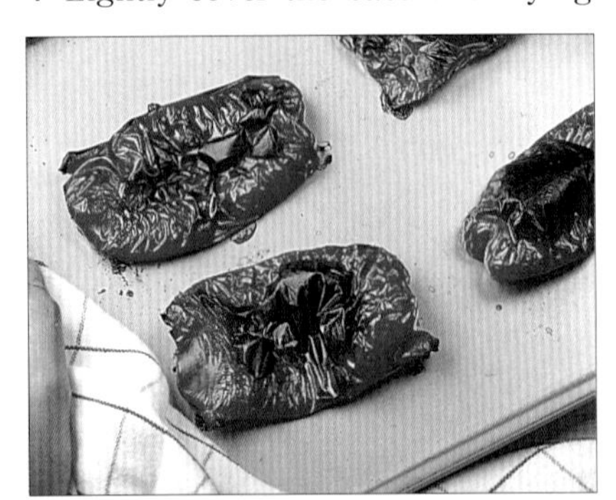

Cook the capsicum under a hot grill until the skin blackens and blisters.

Add the olive oil and blend until the pesto is smooth.

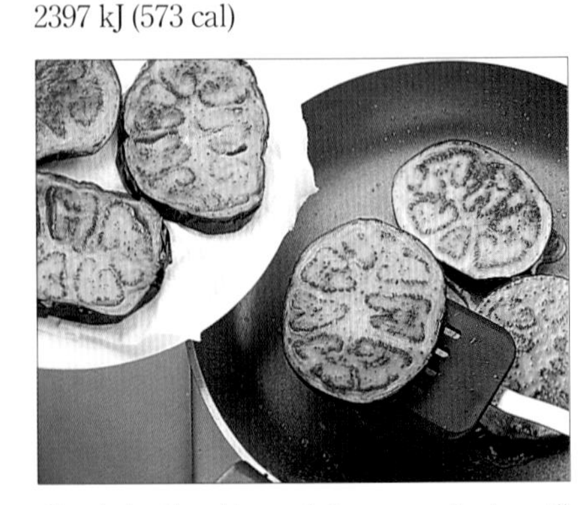

Cook both sides of the eggplant until golden, then drain on paper towels.

MEDITERRANEAN RICOTTA TARTS

Preparation time: 20 minutes + 20 minutes cooling
Total cooking time: 30 minutes
Serves 4 as an entrée

1/3 cup (35 g) dry breadcrumbs
2 tablespoons virgin olive oil
1 clove garlic, crushed
1/2 red capsicum, quartered and cut into 5 mm wide strips
1 zucchini, cut into 5 cm x 5 mm strips
2 slices prosciutto, chopped
375 g firm ricotta (see Note)
1/3 cup (40 g) grated Cheddar
1/3 cup (35 g) grated Parmesan
2 tablespoons shredded fresh basil
4 black olives, pitted and sliced

1 Preheat the oven to moderate 180°C (350°F/Gas 4). Lightly grease four 8 cm (2.5 cm deep) fluted tart tins. Lightly sprinkle 1 teaspoon of the breadcrumbs on the base and side of each tin.
2 To make the topping, heat half the oil in a frying pan, add the garlic, capsicum and zucchini and cook, stirring, over medium heat for 5 minutes, or until the vegetables are soft. Remove from the heat and add the prosciutto. Season to taste with salt and cracked black pepper.
3 Place the ricotta in a large bowl and add the cheeses and remaining breadcrumbs. Season. Press the mixture into the tins and smooth the surface. Sprinkle with basil.
4 Scatter the topping over the ricotta mixture, top with the olives, then drizzle with the remaining oil.
5 Bake for 20 minutes, or until the tarts are slightly puffed and golden around the edges. Cool completely (the tarts will deflate on cooling) and carefully remove from the tins. Do not refrigerate.

NUTRITION PER SERVE
Protein 20 g; Fat 27 g; Carbohydrate 8 g; Dietary Fibre 1 g; Cholesterol 66 mg; 1457 kJ (348 cal)

COOK'S FILE

NOTE: Use firm ricotta or very well-drained ricotta, or the tarts will be difficult to remove from the tins.

Sprinkle breadcrumbs over the base and side of each tin.

Cook the vegetables in a frying pan over medium heat until soft.

Press the ricotta mixture into the tins, then smooth the surface.

Bake the tarts until they are puffed and golden around the edges.

Antipasto and meze platters

When you're entertaining, make your life easier by dropping into your local deli or supermarket to choose from the huge range of pre-prepared goodies. You can create sumptuous food platters for a few guests or a whole party. Antipasti are delicacies of Italian origin and meze are other morsels, usually from Greece, Turkey and Lebanon—keep them separate or mix them as you like.

ANTIPASTO

Olives: large, small, black, green, stuffed, marinated or plain—there is a huge variety to choose from!

Vegetables: marinated artichoke hearts; sun-dried, semi-dried, oven-roasted or vine-ripened tomatoes; grilled capsicum, eggplant or zucchini slices; marinated mushrooms; roasted caramelised baby onions; lightly blanched asparagus spears.

Toppings: pesto (preferably basil or sun-dried tomato), tapenade (olive paste), artichoke purée and porcini paste are all great on bread.

Cold sliced Italian meats: salami, prosciutto, mortadella, ham and pepperoni are just a few of them.

Cheese: try mozzarella, bocconcini, gorgonzola, fontina, provolone, pecorino and Parmesan.

Seafood: anchovies; mussels; calamari rings; tuna. Add some chopped basil, garlic, a little olive oil and a squeeze of lemon.

Fruit: figs (fresh or dried); grapes; melon. Wedges of melon are great with prosciutto wrapped around them.

Breads: Try focaccia, grissini, or brush a little olive oil over some slices of wood-fired bread, rub with garlic and grill for fabulous bruschetta.

MEZE

Olives: look for either marinated or plain Kalamata olives (black–purple, almond shaped olives).

Dips: tzatziki (cucumber and yoghurt); hummus (chickpea and tahini); taramasalata (fish roe); baba ganouj (eggplant); carrot, beetroot or spinach with yoghurt; skordalia (potato, garlic and almonds).

Breads: serve chunks or slices of pide (Turkish bread), pitta bread rounds, Lebanese bread or any other flat bread to scoop up the dips, eat with cheese or just serve with olive oil.

Seafood: calamari; marinated baby octopus; prawns; sardines. Serve with a bowl of freshly cut lemon wedges—they give a zing to the seafood and a burst of colour to the table.

Cheese: feta (a crumbly, salty cheese traditionally made from sheep's milk); kefalotyri (a salty, hard Greek ewe's or goat's milk cheese); haloumi (a hard, salty sheep's milk cheese). Try marinating some haloumi in olive oil and fresh herbs and, if you are adventurous, cook on a hot barbecue until browned on both sides.

Other bite-size bits: dolmades (stuffed vine leaves); falafel (herbed chickpea patties); kibbeh (cracked wheat and minced meat); spanokopita (spinach and feta triangles).

LEMON AND HERB RISOTTO WITH FRIED MUSHROOMS

Preparation time: 30 minutes
Total cooking time: 45 minutes
Serves 4

Risotto
1 litre chicken or vegetable stock
pinch saffron threads
2 tablespoons olive oil
2 leeks, thinly sliced
2 cloves garlic, crushed
2 cups (440 g) arborio rice
2–3 teaspoons finely grated lemon rind
2–3 tablespoons lemon juice
2 tablespoons chopped fresh flat-leaf parsley
2 tablespoons snipped fresh chives
2 tablespoons chopped fresh oregano
70 g grated Parmesan
100 g mascarpone

Fried mushrooms
30 g butter
1 tablespoon virgin olive oil
200 g small flat mushrooms, cut into thick slices
1 tablespoon balsamic vinegar

1 Bring the stock and saffron threads to the boil in a saucepan. Reduce the heat, cover and keep at a low simmer.
2 Heat the olive oil in a large saucepan over medium heat. Add the leek, cook for 5 minutes, then add the garlic and cook for a further 5 minutes, or until golden. Add the rice and stir for 1 minute, or until well coated with the oil.
3 Add half the lemon rind and juice, then add 1/2 cup (125 ml) of the hot stock. Stir constantly over medium heat until all the liquid has been absorbed. Continue adding more stock, 1/2 cup (125 ml) at a time, stirring constantly, for 25 minutes, or until the stock is absorbed and the rice is tender and creamy.
4 Stir in the parsley, chives, oregano, Parmesan, mascarpone and the remaining lemon rind and lemon juice, then remove from the heat, cover and keep warm.
5 To cook the mushrooms, melt the butter and virgin olive oil in a large frying pan, add the mushroom slices and vinegar and cook, stirring, over high heat for 5–7 minutes, or until the mushrooms are tender and all the liquid has been absorbed.
6 Serve the risotto in large bowls topped with the mushrooms. Garnish with sprigs of fresh herbs, if desired.

NUTRITION PER SERVE
Protein 20 g; Fat 30 g; Carbohydrate 90 g; Dietary Fibre 6 g; Cholesterol 60 mg; 3012 kJ (720 cal)

Stir the leek and garlic until the leek is lightly golden.

Stir constantly until the stock is absorbed and the rice is creamy.

VEGETARIAN PIZZAS

Preparation time: 30 minutes
Total cooking time: 50 minutes
Serves 4

6 Roma tomatoes, halved lengthways
1/4 cup (60 ml) olive oil
sea salt flakes, to sprinkle
3 whole marinated artichoke hearts
1 cup (50 g) firmly packed fresh basil
2 cloves garlic, crushed
2 tablespoons pine nuts
1/3 cup (35 g) grated Parmesan
4 ready-made 17 cm pizza bases
160 g haloumi cheese, sliced lengthways into twelve 5 mm slices
12 Kalamata olives
1 cup (25 g) shredded rocket

1 Preheat the oven to hot 210°C (415°F/Gas 6–7). Place the tomatoes, cut-side-up, on a baking tray. Drizzle with 1 tablespoon of the oil and season with sea salt and pepper. Bake for 35 minutes. Remove from the oven, but leave the oven on.
2 Cut the artichoke hearts into quarters, reserving 1 tablespoon of the marinade.
3 To make the pesto, place the basil, garlic, pine nuts and Parmesan in a small food processor or blender and process until roughly chopped. With the motor running, slowly pour in the remaining olive oil until you have a smooth paste.
4 Spread the pesto evenly over each pizza base, leaving a 1 cm border. Arrange three tomato halves and three artichoke quarters on top of each pizza.
5 Pour the reserved marinade over the haloumi, then place three slices of haloumi on each pizza. Top with the olives and bake for 15 minutes, or until the base is crisp. Garnish with the rocket and serve.

NUTRITION PER SERVE
Protein 22 g; Fat 34 g; Carbohydrate 18 g; Dietary Fibre 5 g; Cholesterol 35 mg; 1945 kJ (465 cal)

Drizzle the tomatoes with oil and season with salt and black pepper.

Add the oil and process until the pesto is a smooth paste.

Arrange the artichokes, tomatoes and haloumi over the pesto.

COCONUT PRAWNS WITH CHILLI DRESSING

Preparation time: 35 minutes + 30 minutes refrigeration
Total cooking time: 30 minutes
Serves 4 as an entrée

24 raw king prawns, peeled and deveined, with tails left intact
plain flour, to coat
1 egg
1 tablespoon milk
1 cup (60 g) shredded coconut
1/2 cup (25 g) chopped fresh coriander leaves
2 1/2 tablespoons oil
300 g red Asian shallots, chopped
2 cloves garlic, finely chopped
2 teaspoons finely chopped fresh ginger
1 red chilli, seeds and membrane removed, thinly sliced
1 teaspoon ground turmeric
270 ml coconut cream
2 kaffir lime leaves, thinly sliced
2 teaspoons lime juice
2 teaspoons palm sugar
3 teaspoons fish sauce
oil, for shallow-frying
1 tablespoon chopped fresh coriander leaves, extra
150 g mixed lettuce leaves

1 Holding the prawns by their tails, coat them in flour, then dip them into the combined egg and milk and then in the combined coconut and coriander. Refrigerate for 30 minutes.
2 Heat the oil in a saucepan and cook the shallots, garlic, ginger, chilli and turmeric over medium heat for 3–5 minutes, or until fragrant. Add the cream, lime leaves, lime juice, sugar and fish sauce. Bring to the boil, then reduce the heat and simmer for 2–3 minutes, or until thick. Keep warm.
3 Heat 2 cm oil in a frying pan and cook the prawns in batches for 3–5 minutes, or until golden. Drain on paper towels and season with salt.
4 Add the extra coriander to the dressing. Divide the lettuce among four bowls, top with the prawns and drizzle with the dressing.

NUTRITION PER SERVE
Protein 7.5 g; Fat 47 g; Carbohydrate 12 g; Dietary Fibre 5 g; Cholesterol 55 mg; 2060 kJ (490 cal)

Peel and devein the prawns, keeping the tails intact.

Dip the floured prawns into the egg, then in the coriander mixture.

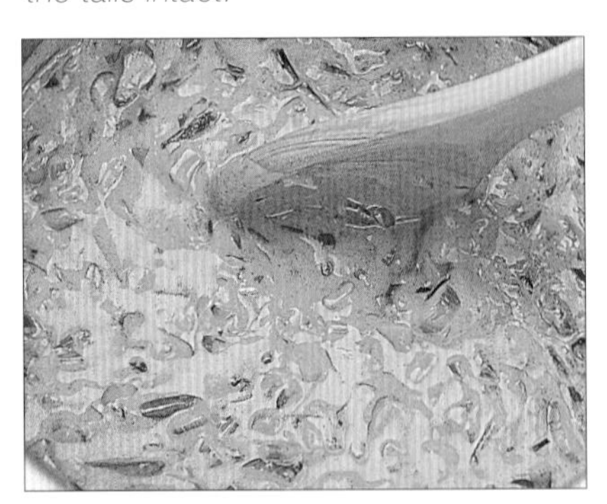

Simmer the dressing until it becomes quite thick.

Cook the prawns in batches until golden, then drain on paper towels.

CHARGRILLED BABY OCTOPUS SALAD

Preparation time: 30 minutes + 2 hours refrigeration
Total cooking time: 15 minutes
Serves 4 as an entrée

- 1 kg baby octopus
- 1 teaspoon sesame oil
- 2 tablespoons lime juice
- 2 tablespoons fish sauce
- 1/4 cup (60 ml) sweet chilli sauce
- 200 g mixed salad leaves
- 1 red capsicum, very thinly sliced
- 2 small Lebanese cucumbers, seeded and cut into ribbons
- 4 red Asian shallots, chopped
- 100 g toasted unsalted peanuts, chopped

1 To clean the octopus, remove the head from the tentacles by cutting just underneath the eyes. To clean the head, carefully slit the head open and remove the gut. Cut it in half. Push out the beak from the centre of the tentacles, then cut the tentacles into sets of four or two, depending on their size. Pull the skin away from the head and tentacles if it comes away easily. The eyes will come off as you pull off the skin.

2 To make the marinade, combine the sesame oil, lime juice, fish sauce and sweet chilli sauce in a shallow non-metallic bowl. Add the octopus, and stir to coat. Cover and refrigerate for 2 hours.

3 Heat a chargrill pan or barbecue to very hot. Drain the octopus, reserving the marinade, then cook in batches for 3–5 minutes, turning occasionally.

4 Pour the marinade into a small saucepan, bring to the boil and cook for 2 minutes, or until it has slightly thickened.

5 Divide the salad leaves among four plates, scatter with capsicum and cucumber, then top with the octopus. Drizzle with the marinade and sprinkle with the red Asian shallots and peanuts.

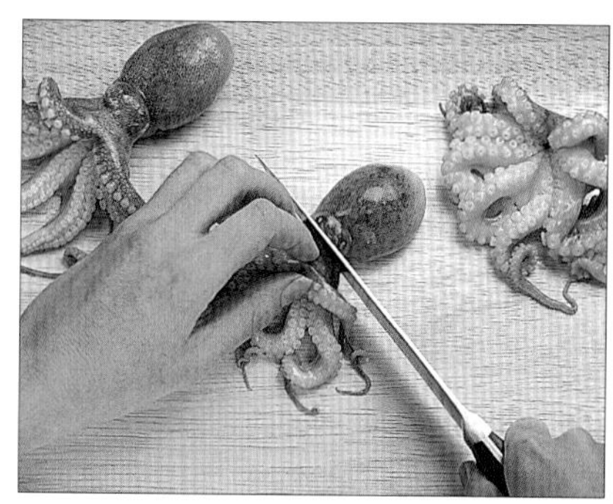

Remove the head from the tentacles by cutting just underneath the eyes.

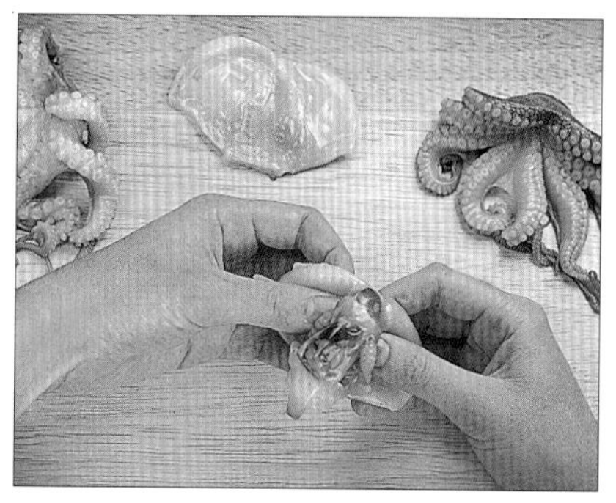

To clean the head, slit the head open and remove the gut.

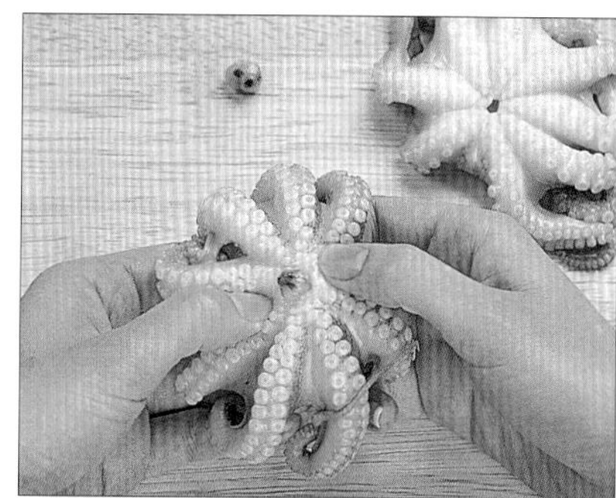

Push the beak out from the centre of the tentacles.

Pull the skin away from the head and tentacles if it comes away easily.

NUTRITION PER SERVE
Protein 50 g; Fat 17 g; Carbohydrate 9 g; Dietary Fibre 5 g; Cholesterol 500 mg; 1622 kJ (387 cal)

ASPARAGUS WITH POACHED QUAIL EGGS AND LIME HOLLANDAISE

Preparation time: 15 minutes
Total cooking time: 10 minutes
Serves 4 as an entrée

32 asparagus spears
2 tablespoons virgin olive oil
2 teaspoons cracked black pepper
2 teaspoons white vinegar
12 quail eggs
2 egg yolks
150 g butter, melted
2 tablespoons lime juice
paprika, to serve
shavings of good-quality Parmesan, to serve

1 Trim the asparagus, brush with a little of the oil, then roll in the pepper, shaking off any excess.

2 Half fill a deep frying pan with water and bring to a gentle simmer, then add the vinegar—this will stop the egg white separating from the yolk as it cooks. Crack a quail egg into a small bowl before gently sliding it into the pan. Repeat with the other eggs. (You will probably need to cook them in two batches.) Cook for 1–2 minutes, or until the egg white turns opaque, then carefully remove from the pan with an egg slide and keep warm.

3 Heat the remaining oil in a large frying pan and cook the asparagus over high heat for 2–3 minutes, or until tender and bright green.

4 To make the hollandaise, place the egg yolks in a blender or whisk by hand and slowly add the melted butter in a thin, steady stream. Mix until all the butter has been added and the mixture has thickened slightly. Add the lime juice, season to taste with salt and cracked black pepper, then mix well.

5 Divide the asparagus among four warmed serving plates, top with three quail eggs per person, drizzle with some of the hollandaise and sprinkle with paprika and Parmesan shavings. Best served immediately.

NUTRITION PER SERVE
Protein 30 g; Fat 50 g; Carbohydrate 2 g; Dietary Fibre 1 g; Cholesterol 425 mg; 2933 kJ (701 cal)

Trim the asparagus, brush with oil and roll in cracked black pepper.

Gently slide each cracked quail egg into simmering water, one at a time.

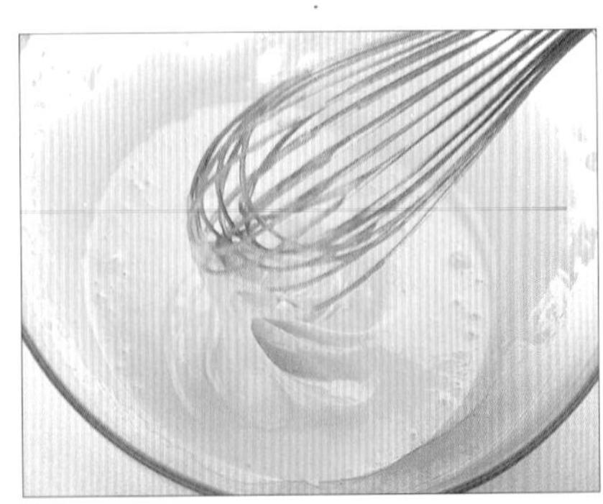

Whisk the egg yolks and butter together until slightly thickened.

SAFFRON PASTA WITH GARLIC PRAWNS AND PRESERVED LEMON

Preparation time: 20 minutes
Total cooking time: 20 minutes
Serves 4

1/2 cup (125 ml) dry white wine
pinch saffron threads
500 g fresh saffron or plain angel-hair pasta
1 tablespoon virgin olive oil
30 g butter
750 g raw prawns, peeled and deveined
3 cloves garlic, crushed
100 g butter, for pan-frying, extra
1/2 preserved lemon, rinsed, pith and flesh removed, cut into thin strips
1 tablespoon lemon juice
4 spring onions, thinly sliced
4 kaffir lime leaves, thinly shredded
1/2 cup (125 ml) chicken stock
2 tablespoons snipped fresh chives

1 Place the wine and saffron in a small saucepan and boil for 3 minutes, or until reduced by half. Remove from the heat.
2 Cook the pasta in a large saucepan of boiling water for 2–3 minutes, or until *al dente*. Drain and keep warm.
3 Heat the oil and butter in a large frying pan and cook the prawns in batches over high heat for 3 minutes, or until pink and tender. Cut into thirds, then transfer to a plate and keep warm.
4 Add the garlic and extra butter to the same pan and cook over medium heat for 3 minutes, or until golden. Add the wine and stir to remove any sediment from the bottom of the pan. Add the preserved lemon, lemon juice, spring onion, lime leaves and stock and bring to the boil, then reduce the heat and simmer for 2 minutes.
5 Return the prawns to the frying pan and heat through. Serve the pasta in mounds, then top with some of the prawns and sauce and sprinkle with snipped fresh chives.

NUTRITION PER SERVE
Protein 15 g; Fat 27 g; Carbohydrate 90 g; Dietary Fibre 7.5 g; Cholesterol 64 mg; 2888 kJ (690 cal)

Cook the pasta in a large saucepan until al dente, then drain well.

Cook the prawns in batches until pink and tender.

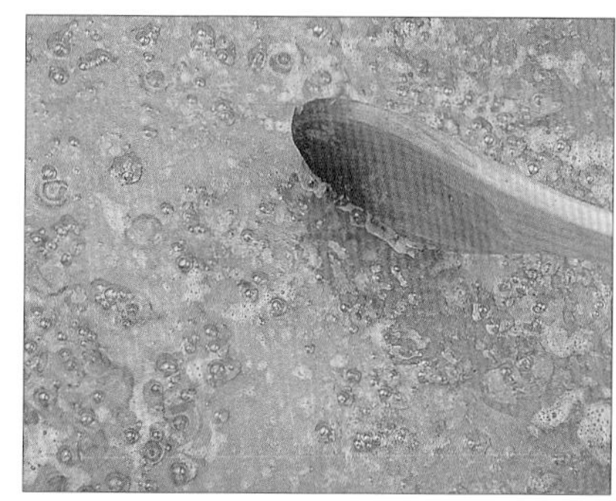

Stir to remove any sediment from the bottom of the pan.

OYSTERS WITH FOUR TOPPINGS

Preparation time: 25 minutes
Total cooking time: 10 minutes
Serves 4 as an entrée

48 freshly shucked oysters (e.g. Pacific) (see Note)
rock salt, to serve

Tomato and coriander salsa (cold)
2 small vine-ripened tomatoes
40 g finely chopped red onion
1 tablespoon finely chopped fresh coriander leaves
1 tablespoon rice vinegar
1/2 teaspoon caster sugar

To make the tomato and coriander salsa, cut the tomatoes in half and remove the seeds with a teaspoon. Finely dice the tomato flesh and place in a small bowl with the red onion and chopped coriander leaves. Mix together well. Combine the rice vinegar and caster sugar in a jug, then stir into the tomato salsa. Season to taste with salt and cracked black pepper and refrigerate until ready to serve on the oysters.

Black bean topping (warm)
1 1/2 tablespoons canned salted black beans
2 teaspoons peanut oil
1 clove garlic, crushed
1 spring onion, finely sliced
3 teaspoons dark soy sauce
3 teaspoons sherry
finely chopped red capsicum, to serve

To make the black bean topping, thoroughly wash the black beans under running water to remove any excess salt, then drain them. Roughly chop the beans and set aside. Heat the peanut oil in a small saucepan over medium heat, add the garlic and spring onion and cook for 30 seconds before adding the dark soy sauce, sherry and black beans. Simmer, stirring, for 2 minutes, or until the sauce has slightly thickened, then season to taste with salt and cracked black pepper. This topping is best served while warm.

Chilli and lime sauce (cold)
1 teaspoon peanut oil
1 clove garlic, crushed
2 teaspoons lime juice
1 tablespoon sweet chilli sauce
1/2 teaspoon sesame oil
1 teaspoon fish sauce
finely chopped Lebanese cucumber, to serve

To make the chilli and lime sauce, heat the peanut oil in a small saucepan, add the garlic and cook for 1 minute, or until softened. Stir in the lime juice, sweet chilli sauce, sesame oil and fish sauce and simmer for a minute, or until just thickened. Allow to cool completely before serving.

Ginger and spring onion topping (warm)
1 tablespoon Japanese soy sauce
2 teaspoons rice vinegar
3 teaspoons mirin
2 teaspoons thin strips fresh ginger
2 spring onions, thinly sliced on the diagonal

To make the ginger and spring onion topping, combine the soy sauce, rice vinegar and mirin in a small saucepan and simmer over low heat for 1 minute. Add the ginger and spring onion and simmer for a further 2 minutes. Serve warm.

To serve, sprinkle rock salt liberally on four plates. Place twelve oysters on each plate. Top three of the oysters on each plate with the tomato and coriander salsa. Spoon the black bean topping over another three, then sprinkle them with finely chopped red capsicum. Spoon chilli and lime sauce over three more of the oysters and top with finely chopped cucumber. Drizzle the ginger and spring onion topping over the remaining three oysters. Serve immediately.

NUTRITION PER SERVE
Protein 5 g; Fat 4 g; Carbohydrate 4 g; Dietary Fibre 1 g; Cholesterol 24 mg; 320 kJ (77 cal)

COOK'S FILE

NOTE: When buying fresh oysters, look for plump moist ones. The flesh should be creamy with a clear liquid surrounding it. They should smell like the sea and have no shell particles.

Tomato and coriander salsa
Cut the tomatoes in half and remove the seeds with a teaspoon.

Black bean topping
Simmer the black bean mixture until slightly thickened.

Chilli and lime sauce
Simmer the chilli and lime mixture until just thickened.

Ginger and spring onion topping
Add the ginger and spring onion and simmer for 2 minutes.

CARAMELISED ONION, ROCKET AND BLUE CHEESE TARTS

Preparation time: 30 minutes + 30 minutes refrigeration
Total cooking time: 1 hour 10 minutes
Serves 6

Pastry
2 cups (250 g) plain flour
125 g butter, chilled and cut into cubes
1/4 cup (25 g) finely grated Parmesan
1 egg, lightly beaten
1/4 cup (60 ml) chilled water

Filling
2 tablespoons olive oil
3 onions, thinly sliced
100 g baby rocket leaves
100 g blue cheese, lightly crumbled
3 eggs, lightly beaten
1/4 cup (60 ml) cream
1/2 cup (50 g) finely grated Parmesan
pinch grated fresh nutmeg

1 To make the pastry, sift the flour into a large bowl and add the butter. Rub the butter into the flour with your fingertips until it resembles fine breadcrumbs. Stir in the Parmesan.
2 Make a well in the centre of the dry ingredients, add the egg and water and mix with a flat-bladed knife, using a cutting action, until the mixture comes together in beads.
3 Gently gather the dough together and lift out onto a lightly floured work surface. Press into a ball and flatten it slightly into a disc, wrap in plastic wrap and refrigerate for 30 minutes.
4 Preheat the oven to moderately hot 200°C (400°F/Gas 6). Divide the pastry into six. Roll the dough out between two sheets of baking paper to fit six round 8 cm (3 cm deep) fluted loose-bottomed tart tins, remove the top sheet of paper and invert the pastry into the tins. Use a small ball of pastry to help press the pastry into the tins, allowing any excess to hang over the sides. Roll the rolling pin over the tins to cut off any excess.
5 Line the pastry shells with a piece of crumpled baking paper that is large enough to cover the base and side of each tin and pour in some baking beads or (uncooked) rice. Bake for 10 minutes, then remove the paper and baking beads and return the pastry to the oven for 10 minutes, or until the base is dry and golden. Cool slightly. Reduce the oven to moderate 180°C (350°F/Gas 4).
6 Heat the oil in a large frying pan, add the onion and cook over medium heat for 20 minutes, or until the onion is caramelised. (Don't rush this step.)
7 Add the rocket and stir until wilted. Remove from the pan and cool.
8 Divide the onion mixture among the tart bases, then sprinkle with the blue cheese. Whisk together the eggs, cream, Parmesan and nutmeg and pour evenly over each of the tarts. Place on a baking tray and bake for 20–30 minutes. Serve either hot or cold with a mixed green salad.

NUTRITION PER SERVE
Protein 18 g; Fat 40 g; Carbohydrate 33 g; Dietary Fibre 2.5 g; Cholesterol 215 mg; 2388 kJ (570 cal)

Rub the butter into the flour until it resembles fine breadcrumbs.

Use a small ball of pastry to press the pastry into the tins.

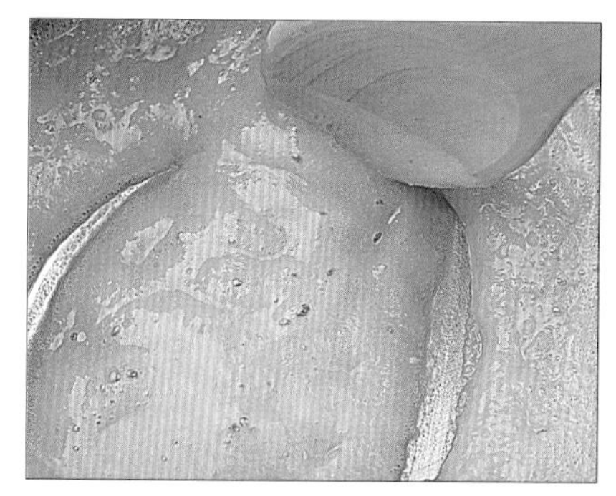

Cook the butter and flour mixture until it is golden.

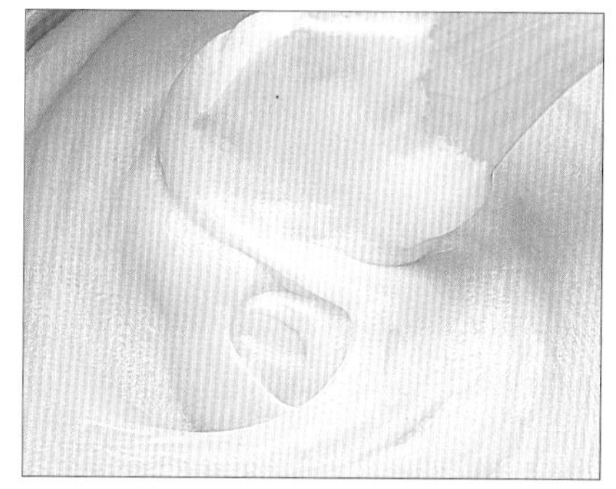

Stir the mixture constantly until it boils and thickens.

Using a balloon whisk, beat the egg whites until soft peaks form.

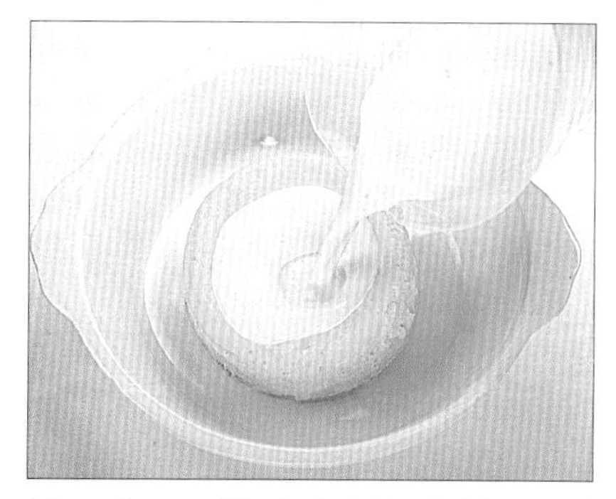

Place the soufflés in individual dishes and pour on the cream.

TWICE-BAKED CHEESE SOUFFLES

Preparation time: 30 minutes + 10 minutes standing + refrigeration
Total cooking time: 45 minutes
Serves 4 as an entrée

1 cup (250 ml) milk
2 cloves
1 onion, halved
3 black peppercorns
1 bay leaf
60 g butter
1/4 cup (30 g) self-raising flour
2 eggs, at room temperature, separated
125 g Gruyère cheese, grated
1 cup (250 ml) cream
1/2 cup (50 g) grated Parmesan

1 Preheat the oven to moderate 180°C (350°F/Gas 4). Grease four 1/2 cup (125 ml) ramekins. Put the milk, clove-studded onion, peppercorns and bay leaf in a saucepan and heat until just about to boil, then remove from the heat and leave for 10 minutes. Strain.
2 Melt the butter in a saucepan, add the flour and cook over medium heat for 1 minute, or until golden. Remove from the heat and gradually stir in the milk, then return to the heat and stir constantly until the mixture boils and thickens. Simmer for 1 minute.
3 Transfer to a bowl, add the egg yolks and Gruyère cheese and mix.
4 Beat the egg whites in a clean dry bowl with a balloon whisk until soft peaks form, then gently fold into the milk mixture. Divide among the ramekins and run your finger around the rim to help the soufflés rise. Place the ramekins in a roasting tin with enough boiling water to come halfway up the sides of the dishes. Bake for 15–20 minutes, or until puffed. Remove, cool, then refrigerate for up to 2 days.
5 To serve, preheat the oven to moderately hot 200°C (400°F/Gas 6), remove the soufflés from the ramekins and place each in a shallow ovenproof dish, pour the cream over the top, sprinkle with Parmesan and bake for 20 minutes, or until golden.

NUTRITION PER SERVE
Protein 22 g; Fat 55 g; Carbohydrate 12 g; Dietary Fibre 0 g; Cholesterol 262 mg; 2672 kJ (638 cal)

SPICED LENTIL SOUP

Preparation time: 10 minutes + 20 minutes standing
Total cooking time: 50 minutes
Serves 4

1 eggplant
1/4 cup (60 ml) olive oil
1 onion, finely chopped
2 teaspoons brown mustard seeds
2 teaspoons ground cumin
1 teaspoon garam masala
1/4 teaspoon cayenne pepper (optional)
2 large carrots, cut into cubes
1 celery stick, diced
400 g can crushed tomatoes
1 cup (110 g) puy lentils
1 litre chicken stock
3/4 cup (35 g) roughly chopped fresh coriander leaves
1/2 cup (125 g) Greek-style plain yoghurt

1 Cut the eggplant into cubes, place in a colander, sprinkle with salt and leave for 20 minutes. Rinse well and pat dry with paper towels.
2 Heat the oil in a large saucepan over medium heat. Add the onion and cook for 5 minutes, or until soft. Add the eggplant, stir to coat in oil and cook for 3 minutes, or until softened.
3 Add all the spices and cook, stirring, for 1 minute, or until fragrant and the mustard seeds begin to pop. Add the carrot and celery and cook for 1 minute. Stir in the tomato, lentils and stock and bring to the boil. Reduce the heat and simmer for 40 minutes, or until the lentils are tender and the liquid is reduced to a thick stew-like soup. Season to taste with salt and cracked black pepper.
4 Stir the coriander into the soup just before serving. Ladle the soup into four warmed bowls and serve with a dollop of the yoghurt on top.

NUTRITION PER SERVE
Protein 11 g; Fat 16 g; Carbohydrate 20 g; Dietary Fibre 8.5 g; Cholesterol 5 mg; 1148 kJ (274 cal)

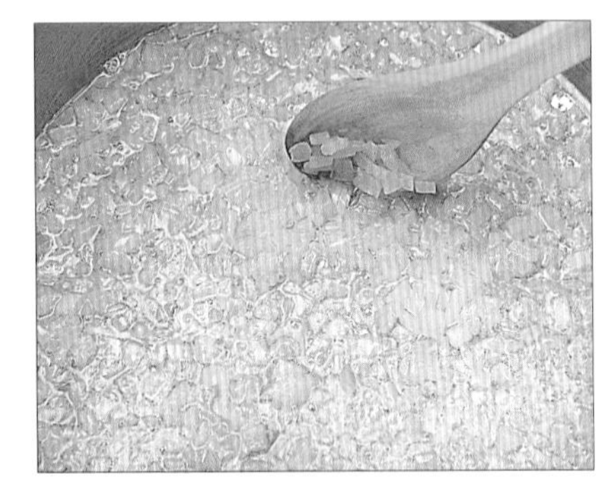

Cook the chopped onion in a large saucepan until soft.

Add the spices to the vegetables and stir until fragrant.

Simmer the mixture until thick and the lentils are tender.

TANDOORI CHICKEN PIZZA

Preparation time: 15 minutes + 2 hours refrigeration
Total cooking time: 30 minutes
Serves 4

1/2 cup (125 g) plain yoghurt
1 tablespoon tandoori paste
2 chicken breast fillets
1 tablespoon oil
1/2 cup (125 g) tomato paste
1 clove garlic, crushed
1 teaspoon caster sugar
1/2 teaspoon ground cumin
1/4 teaspoon ground coriander
3 teaspoons chopped fresh mint
1/3 cup (90 g) plain yoghurt, extra
1/2 teaspoon caster sugar, extra
4 ready-made individual soft, thick pizza bases
1 small red onion, thinly sliced into rings
2 tablespoons mango chutney
1 1/2 tablespoons flaked almonds, toasted
3 tablespoons roughly chopped fresh coriander leaves
snow pea sprouts, to garnish (optional)

1 Combine the yoghurt and tandoori paste in a bowl, then add the chicken and toss well. Cover and refrigerate for 2 hours. Preheat the oven to moderately hot 200°C (400°F/Gas 6).

2 Preheat a chargrill pan and brush with oil. Cook the chicken on medium heat for 3–4 minutes each side, or until brown but not cooked through.

3 Place the tomato paste, garlic, sugar, cumin and ground coriander in a bowl and stir together well. Combine the mint, extra yoghurt and extra sugar in a separate bowl.

4 Slice the chicken into strips on the diagonal. Spread the tomato mixture over the pizza bases, leaving a 1 cm border, then sprinkle with onion rings and chicken strips. Bake for 15–20 minutes, then top with the minted yoghurt, chutney, almonds, fresh coriander and snow pea sprouts. Serve immediately.

NUTRITION PER SERVE
Protein 26 g; Fat 9.5 g; Carbohydrate 13 g; Dietary Fibre 2 g; Cholesterol 60 mg; 1030 kJ (245 cal)

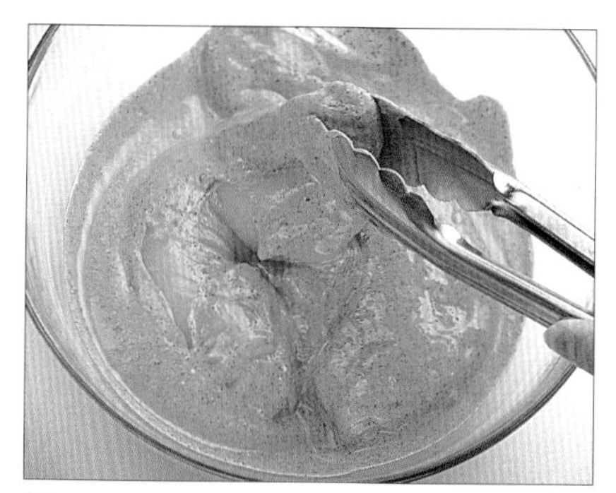

Toss the chicken breasts in the tandoori paste mixture.

Chargrill the chicken until browned but not cooked through.

Spread the bases with tomato paste, then top with onion and chicken.

SCALLOPS ON ASIAN RISOTTO CAKES

Preparation time: 35 minutes + 3 hours 10 minutes refrigeration
Total cooking time: 40 minutes
Serves 4 as an entrée

2 cups (500 ml) vegetable stock
2 tablespoons mirin
1 stem lemon grass (white part only), bruised
2 kaffir lime leaves
3 fresh coriander roots
2 tablespoons fish sauce
1 tablespoon butter
2–3 tablespoons peanut oil
3 red Asian shallots, thinly sliced
4 spring onions, chopped
3 cloves garlic, chopped
2 tablespoons finely chopped fresh ginger
1 1/4 teaspoons white pepper
2/3 cup (140 g) arborio rice
2 tablespoons toasted unsalted chopped peanuts
1 cup (50 g) chopped fresh coriander leaves
2 cloves garlic, chopped, extra
1 teaspoon finely chopped fresh ginger, extra
1/4 cup (60 ml) lime juice
1–2 teaspoons grated palm sugar
vegetable oil, for pan-frying
plain flour, to dust
1 tablespoon vegetable oil, extra
16 large white scallops without roe, beard removed

1 Heat the stock, mirin, lemon grass, lime leaves, coriander roots, half the fish sauce and 1 cup (250 ml) water in a saucepan, bring to the boil, then reduce the heat and keep at a low simmer.

2 Heat the butter and 1 tablespoon of the peanut oil in a large saucepan over medium heat until bubbling. Add the shallots, spring onion, garlic, ginger and 1 teaspoon of the white pepper and cook for 2–3 minutes, or until fragrant and the onion is soft. Stir in the rice and toss until well coated.

3 Add 1/2 cup (125 ml) of the stock (avoid the lemon grass and coriander roots). Stir constantly over medium heat until nearly all the liquid is absorbed. Continue adding the stock 1/2 cup (125 ml) at a time, stirring constantly, for 20–25 minutes, or until all the stock is absorbed and the rice is tender and creamy. Remove from the heat, cool, then cover and refrigerate for 3 hours, or until cold.

4 To make the pesto, combine the peanuts, coriander, extra garlic and ginger and the remaining pepper in a blender or food processor and process until finely chopped. With the motor running, slowly add the lime juice, sugar and remaining fish sauce and peanut oil and process until smooth—you might not need all the oil.

5 Divide the risotto into four balls, then mould into patties. Cover and refrigerate for 10 minutes. Heat the oil in a large frying pan over medium heat. Dust the patties with flour and cook in batches for 2 minutes each side, or until crisp. Drain on paper towels. Cover and keep warm.

6 Heat the extra oil in a clean frying pan over high heat. Cook the scallops in batches for 1 minute each side.

7 Serve a cake with four scallops, some pesto and lime wedges, if desired.

NUTRITION PER SERVE
Protein 12 g; Fat 32 g; Carbohydrate 36 g; Dietary Fibre 2 g; Cholesterol 30 mg; 1987 kJ (475 cal)

Stir the rice until the stock is absorbed and the rice is tender and creamy.

Cook the flour-dusted patties until crisp and golden.

WON TON CHICKEN RAVIOLI WITH A THAI DRESSING

Preparation time: 35 minutes
Total cooking time: 15 minutes
Serves 4 as an entrée

400 g chicken mince
2 spring onions, finely chopped
3 kaffir lime leaves, very finely shredded
2 tablespoons sweet chilli sauce
3 tablespoons chopped fresh coriander leaves
1 1/2 teaspoons sesame oil
2 teaspoons grated lime rind
270 g packet won ton wrappers
1/2 cup (125 ml) fish sauce
2 tablespoons grated palm sugar
1 tablespoon peanut oil
1 tablespoon lime juice
finely chopped red chilli, to garnish
chopped fresh coriander leaves, to garnish

1 Combine the mince, spring onion, lime leaves, chilli sauce, coriander, sesame oil and lime rind in a bowl.
2 Place a tablespoon of the mixture in the centre of a won ton wrapper, brush the edges lightly with water and top with another wrapper, pressing down around the edges to stop the ravioli from opening during cooking. Repeat with the remaining filling and wrappers.
3 Cook the ravioli in batches in a large saucepan of boiling water for 5 minutes, or until *al dente* and the chicken mince is cooked, then drain well and place on serving plates.
4 Combine the fish sauce, palm sugar, peanut oil and lime juice in a bowl. Pour over the ravioli and garnish with the chilli and coriander.

NUTRITION PER SERVE
Protein 25 g; Fat 15 g; Carbohydrate 11 g; Dietary Fibre 1 g; Cholesterol 50 mg; 1145 kJ (275 cal)

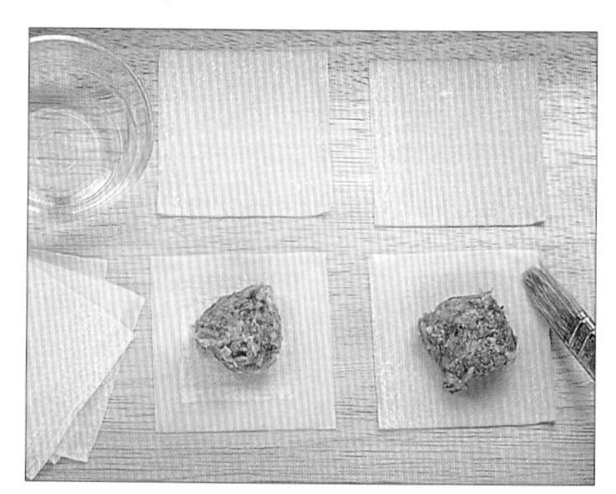

Put a tablespoon of filling on a wrapper and brush the edges with water.

Top with another wrapper and press the edges to seal.

Cook until the mince is cooked and the wrappers are al dente.

Clockwise from left: Rocket and Parmesan salad, Potato and bean salad, Tomato and bocconcini salad, Mesclun with a mustard vinaigrette, Mizuna with sesame dressing, Caesar salad.

Side salads

While these salads may look too good to be relegated to the status of a side dish, they have an important place on the table: simple flavours to complement, but not distract from, the full flavours of the main meals. All the salads serve 4–6 people.

ROCKET AND PARMESAN SALAD

Combine 1/4 cup (60 ml) extra virgin olive oil, 2 tablespoons aged balsamic vinegar, 1 clove crushed garlic and 1 teaspoon brown sugar. Season. Toss the dressing through 200 g baby rocket, then toss in 3/4 cup (75 g) shaved Parmesan. Garnish with extra shaved Parmesan.

CAESAR SALAD

Process 3 eggs, 3 cloves crushed garlic, 2–3 anchovies, 1 teaspoon Worcestershire sauce, 2 tablespoons lime juice and 1 teaspoon Dijon mustard in a food processor until smooth. With the motor running, slowly add 3/4 cup (185 ml) olive oil to produce a creamy dressing. Season. Cut the crusts off 3 slices of white bread, then cut the bread into 1.5 cm cubes. Melt a little butter and olive oil in a frying pan over medium heat, add the bread and cook until crisp. Cook 3 rashers of bacon until crispy, then break into pieces. Combine the leaves from 1 large or 4 baby cos lettuces with as much dressing as you want, then stir in the croutons, bacon and 3/4 cup (75 g) shaved Parmesan.

MIZUNA WITH SESAME DRESSING

Combine 2 tablespoons Japanese ponzu vinegar, 2 teaspoons mirin, 1 tablespoon vegetable oil, 1/2 teaspoon sesame oil, 1 teaspoon finely grated ginger, 1 clove crushed garlic and 1 tablespoon toasted sesame seeds in a small bowl. Toss together 320 g mizuna (Japanese salad greens), 50 g each of julienned daikon and carrot and the dressing. Garnish with extra toasted sesame seeds, if desired.

POTATO AND BEAN SALAD

Cut 4 kipfler or other small waxy potatoes into 5 mm slices and cook in boiling salted water until tender. Drain and set aside. Cut 100 g green beans into 4 cm lengths, blanch, then refresh in iced water, drain and add to the potato. Cut 12 cherry tomatoes in half and combine with the potatoes, beans, 150 g crumbled feta, 1/2 thinly sliced red onion, 1/2 thinly sliced red capsicum and 12 black olives. Combine 2 tablespoons lemon juice, 1 tablespoon red wine vinegar, 1/4 cup (60 ml) virgin olive oil, 2 teaspoons Dijon mustard, 2 cloves crushed garlic and 2 teaspoons each of finely chopped fresh flat-leaf parsley and fresh oregano, then toss through the salad. Garnish with baby capers.

TOMATO AND BOCCONCINI SALAD

Cut 4 Roma tomatoes and 4 pieces of bocconcini (70 g each) into 5 mm slices. Alternate the slices in rows or in a spiral until your ingredients are used up. Tear 8 fresh basil leaves into pieces and scatter over the top. If desired, drizzle with a little extra virgin olive oil and balsamic vinegar and season with sea salt flakes and cracked black pepper.

MESCLUN WITH A MUSTARD VINAIGRETTE

Combine 300 g torn mixed leaves in a large bowl. Whisk together 2 tablespoons extra virgin olive oil, 1 1/2 tablespoons lemon juice, 2 teaspoons Dijon mustard, 1 teaspoon wholegrain mustard, 1 teaspoon sugar and 1 clove crushed garlic in a small bowl and season. Toss the dressing through the leaves, then serve.

SEAFOOD RISOTTO

Preparation time: 30 minutes
Total cooking time: 40 minutes
Serves 4 (6 as an entrée)

12 baby clams
1 1/2 cups (375 ml) white wine
3 1/2 cups vegetable stock
2 bay leaves
1 celery stick, chopped
6 French shallots, chopped
1/4 cup (60 ml) lemon juice
12 raw king prawns, peeled and deveined
12 scallops without roe, beards removed
1 calamari tube, cut into 12 slices
1 tablespoon olive oil
2 tablespoons butter
2/3 cup (80 g) chopped spring onion
4–6 cloves garlic, crushed
1 1/2 tablespoons finely chopped fresh thyme
1 1/2 cups (330 g) arborio rice
1/3 cup (90 g) sour cream
1/3 cup (35 g) grated Parmesan
2 tablespoons chopped fresh flat-leaf parsley
shaved Parmesan, to serve

1 Scrub and rinse the clams to remove any grit, discarding any that are opened or damaged. Place the wine, stock, bay leaves, celery, shallots, lemon juice and 2 1/2 cups (625 ml) water in a saucepan and bring to the boil for 5 minutes. Reduce the heat to a simmer, then add the clams and cook for 3 minutes, or until they open. Using a slotted spoon, transfer the clams to a bowl, discarding any that did not open. Add the prawns to the stock and cook for 2 minutes, or until pink and curled, then transfer to the bowl with the clams. Add the scallops and calamari rings and cook for 1 minute, then transfer to the bowl. Strain the stock, then return to the pan and keep at a low simmer.

2 Heat the oil and half the butter in a large heavy-based saucepan over medium heat. Add the spring onion, garlic and thyme and cook, stirring, for 1 minute. Stir in the rice and cook for 1 minute, or until well coated.

3 Add 1/2 cup (125 ml) of the hot stock. Stir constantly over medium heat until all the stock is absorbed. Continue adding more stock, 1/2 cup (125 ml) at a time, stirring constantly for 25 minutes, or until the stock is absorbed. Add the seafood with the final addition of stock. The rice should be tender and creamy.

4 Remove from the heat and stir in the sour cream, Parmesan and parsley. Season. Serve with shaved Parmesan.

NUTRITION PER SERVE (4)
Protein 43 g; Fat 26 g; Carbohydrate 70 g; Dietary Fibre 3.5 g; Cholesterol 320 mg; 3127 kJ (747 cal)

Cook the clams in the simmering stock until they open.

Cook the prawns until they are pink and curled.

Stir constantly until the stock has been absorbed.

SCALLOPS WITH GOAT'S MILK CHEESE AND CRISPY PROSCIUTTO

Preparation time: 10 minutes
Total cooking time: 10 minutes
Serves 4 as an entrée

4 thin slices prosciutto
16 scallops on shells, roe and beards removed
2–3 tablespoons extra virgin olive oil
1 tablespoon chopped fresh flat-leaf parsley
1/2 teaspoon sea salt flakes
100 g goat's milk cheese, crumbled
2 tablespoons good-quality aged balsamic vinegar

1 Cook the prosciutto under a hot grill until crisp, then drain on paper towels and break into small pieces.
2 Place the scallops on two baking trays. Combine the oil and parsley in a small bowl and season with sea salt and cracked black pepper. Brush the scallops with the oil mixture.
3 Cook the scallops in batches under a hot grill for 2–3 minutes, or until they are tender.
4 Top the scallops with the goat's milk cheese, prosciutto and a drizzle of balsamic vinegar.
5 Carefully transfer the scallops from the trays to serving plates lined with rock salt—the shells will be very hot.

NUTRITION PER SERVE
Protein 11 g; Fat 20 g; Carbohydrate 0 g; Dietary Fibre 0 g; Cholesterol 35 mg; 953 kJ (228 cal)

Roughly break the crisp prosciutto into small pieces.

Brush each of the scallops with the oil mixture.

Cook the scallops under a hot grill until tender.

CARAMELISED PUMPKIN AND RICOTTA LASAGNE WITH LIME BUTTER

Preparation time: 30 minutes
Total cooking time: 30 minutes
Serves 4 as an entrée

1/2 butternut pumpkin (approx. 600 g), peeled and seeded
2 tablespoons olive oil
3 teaspoons finely chopped fresh rosemary
1 teaspoon sea salt flakes
1/4 cup (60 ml) lime juice
1/4 cup (60 ml) white wine
1/4 cup (60 ml) vegetable stock
3 French shallots, finely chopped
1 clove garlic, crushed
1/4 teaspoon white pepper
1 tablespoon cream
150 g butter, chilled and cut into small cubes
2 teaspoons finely diced mustard fruit (see Note)
100 g fresh lasagne sheets, cut into eight 8 cm squares
100 g ricotta
1 amaretti cookie, crushed (optional) (see Note)
small sprigs fresh rosemary, to garnish

1 Preheat the oven to moderately hot 200°C (400°F/Gas 6). Cut the piece of pumpkin in half, then each half into eight slices. Place half the oil, 2 teaspoons of the rosemary and the salt in a bowl and toss the pumpkin slices through the mixture.

2 Put the pumpkin in a single layer on a baking tray and bake for 25–30 minutes, or until cooked and slightly caramelised. Remove from the oven, cover and keep warm.

3 Meanwhile, combine the lime juice, wine, stock, shallots, garlic, white pepper and the remaining rosemary in a small saucepan and simmer for about 15–20 minutes, or until the liquid has reduced to about 2 tablespoons. Strain into a small clean saucepan, then add the cream and simmer for 2–3 minutes, or until thickened slightly. Whisk in the butter a few cubes at a time until all the butter is incorporated and the sauce is thickened, smooth and glossy. Remove from the heat and stir in the mustard fruit. Season and leave covered.

4 Fill a large saucepan with water, add the remaining oil and bring to the boil, then reduce to a simmer. Add the lasagne squares in batches and cook, stirring, for 1–2 minutes, or until *al dente*. Drain well.

5 Gently reheat the pumpkin and the lime butter if necessary. To assemble, place one lasagne square on each plate. Place two slices of pumpkin onto each square, top with one quarter of the ricotta, then top with another two slices of pumpkin and finish with a final layer of lasagne. Give the lime butter a quick whisk, then spoon a little over the top and around the lasagne on the plate. Season. Sprinkle the top of each lasagne with a little of the crushed amaretti and some fresh rosemary.

NUTRITION PER SERVE
Protein 11 g; Fat 16 g; Carbohydrate 34 g; Dietary Fibre 4.5 g; Cholesterol 20 mg; 1413 kJ (340 cal)

COOK'S FILE

NOTE: Mustard fruit is a piquant fruit relish made from crystallised fruits preserved in white wine, honey and mustard. Buy it and amaretti from delicatessens and gourmet food stores.

Cut the piece of pumpkin in half, then cut each half into eight slices.

Bake the pumpkin until cooked through and just caramelised.

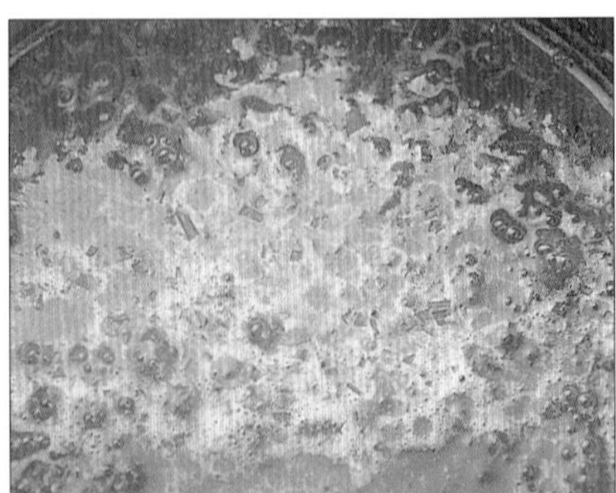

Simmer the liquid until only about 2 tablespoons remain.

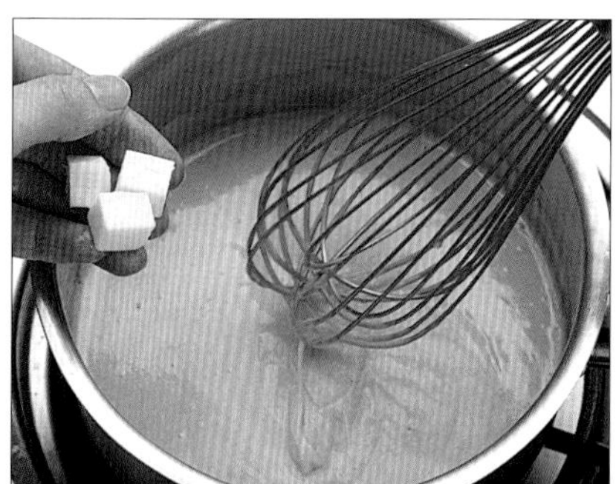

Add a few cubes of butter at a time and whisk until thick and glossy.

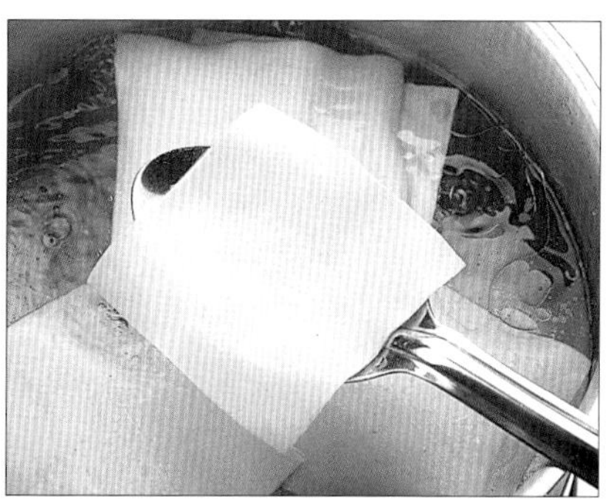

Cook the lasagne squares in batches until al dente.

Spread one quarter of the ricotta over the pumpkin pieces.

TEMPURA PRAWNS WITH SOBA NOODLES AND DASHI BROTH

Preparation time: 20 minutes
Total cooking time: 15 minutes
Serves 4 as an entrée

200 g dried soba noodles
1 spring onion, sliced on the diagonal
1/3 cup (60 g) daikon, cut into thin strips
1 teaspoon dashi granules
1/4 cup (60 ml) Japanese soy sauce
2 tablespoons mirin
1/2 teaspoon caster sugar
2 spring onions, sliced thinly on the diagonal, extra
2 teaspoons black sesame seeds
pickled ginger, to garnish

Tempura prawns
12 raw medium king prawns
oil, for deep-frying
1 cup (125 g) tempura flour
1 cup (250 ml) iced water

1 Bring a large saucepan of water to the boil and cook the noodles for 5 minutes, or until *al dente*. Drain, then add the spring onion and daikon, toss well and keep warm.

2 To make the broth, place the dashi granules, soy sauce, mirin, sugar and 2 cups (500 ml) water in a saucepan and bring to the boil. Reduce the heat and simmer for 2–3 minutes. Remove from the heat, cover and keep warm.

3 To make the tempura prawns, peel and devein the prawns, keeping the tails intact. Make four incisions in the underside of each prawn.

4 Fill a wok or deep heavy-based saucepan one third full of oil and heat until a cube of bread dropped into the oil browns in 15 seconds. Combine the tempura flour with the iced water and mix briefly with chopsticks or a fork—the batter should still be lumpy. Dip each prawn into the batter, leaving the tail uncoated. Deep-fry in batches for about 30 seconds, or until the prawns are light gold, crispy and cooked through. Drain well on crumpled paper towels.

5 Divide the noodles among four bowls and cover with broth, then top with the extra spring onion. Stand three prawns on top and sprinkle with sesame seeds. Garnish with pickled ginger and serve immediately.

NUTRITION PER SERVE
Protein 23 g; Fat 12 g; Carbohydrate 54 g; Dietary Fibre 5 g; Cholesterol 94 mg; 1757 kJ (420 cal)

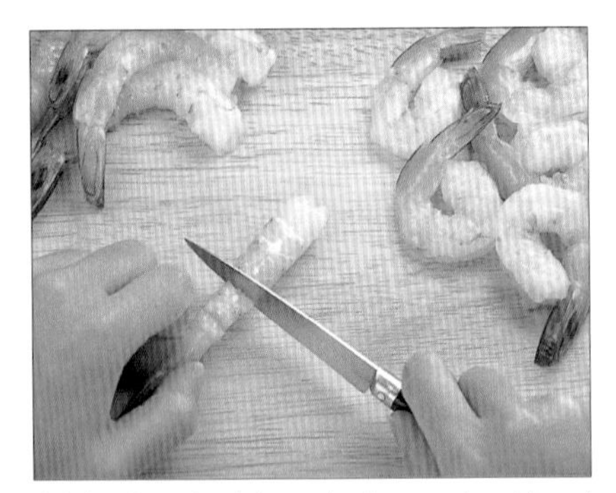

Make four incisions in the underside of each prawn.

Briefly mix the tempura flour and iced water with chopsticks.

Cook the prawns until crisp, lightly golden and cooked through.

SMOKED SALMON SALAD WITH POTATO ROSTI AND HORSERADISH CREAM

Preparation time: 45 minutes
Total cooking time: 30 minutes
Serves 4 as an entrée

1 cup (30 g) watercress sprigs
1 green coral or other loose-leafed lettuce, shredded
100 g baby rocket, trimmed
2 heads of witlof, sliced into 1.5 cm pieces
400 g smoked salmon

Horseradish cream
1/3 cup (80 ml) cream
1/2 red onion, chopped
1 tablespoon lemon juice
1 1/2 tablespoons horseradish

Rösti
1 egg
2 tablespoons plain flour
550 g russet or other starchy potatoes, grated
1/2 cup (80 g) grated onion
2 teaspoons oil
40 g butter

1 Toss all the greens together in a large bowl and set aside.
2 To make the horseradish cream, place the cream, red onion, lemon juice, 1/4 teaspoon salt and 1/4 teaspoon cracked black pepper in a small saucepan and simmer for 2 minutes, or until thickened slightly. Add the horseradish and remove from the heat.
3 To make the rösti, preheat the oven to moderately hot 190°C (375°/Gas 5). Whisk the egg and flour together in a bowl. Squeeze any excess moisture out of the potatoes. Stir the potato into the egg mixture, then add the onion and 1/4 teaspoon each salt and pepper.
4 Heat the oil and butter in a large frying pan over medium heat. Form the potato into four even-sized balls. When the butter begins to brown, add the balls in batches and press down with an egg flip to form 10 cm patties. Cook for 4–5 minutes each side, or until deep brown. Transfer to the oven and cook for 5–7 minutes, or until the outside is crusty and the inside is soft.
5 Just before serving, warm the horseradish cream. Arrange a quarter of the smoked salmon on each plate, with the tips of the salmon slices overlapping in the middle. Place a rösti over the salmon and top with a quarter of the greens. Drizzle with horseradish cream and serve.

NUTRITION PER SERVE
Protein 30 g; Fat 26 g; Carbohydrate 28 g; Dietary Fibre 5 g; Cholesterol 147 mg; 1965 kJ (469 cal)

Simmer the horseradish cream until slightly thickened.

Squeeze the excess moisture out of the grated potato.

Using an egg flip, press the balls of potato into 10 cm patties.

MOROCCAN BEEF PIES

Preparation time: 45 minutes +
30 minutes refrigeration
Total cooking time: 1 hour 20 minutes
Serves 4

1 tablespoon oil
2 cloves garlic, crushed
1 onion, cut into thin wedges
2 teaspoons ground cumin
2 teaspoons ground ginger
2 teaspoons paprika
pinch saffron threads
500 g round steak, cut into 2 cm cubes
1 1/2 cups (375 ml) beef stock
1 small cinnamon stick
100 g pitted prunes, halved
2 carrots, sliced
1 teaspoon grated orange rind
2 cups (250 g) plain flour
125 g butter, chilled and cut into cubes
1 egg, lightly beaten
1/4 preserved lemon, rinsed, pith and flesh removed, finely chopped (optional)
200 g thick plain yoghurt

1 Heat the oil in a large saucepan, add the garlic and onion and cook for 3 minutes, or until softened. Add the cumin, ginger, paprika and saffron and stir for 1 minute, or until fragrant. Add the meat and toss until coated in the spices. Add the stock, cinnamon stick, prunes and carrot. Bring to the boil, reduce the heat and simmer, covered, for 30 minutes. Increase the heat to medium, add the orange rind and cook, uncovered, for 20 minutes, or until the liquid has reduced and thickened slightly. Remove the cinnamon stick and cool completely.

2 To make the pastry, sift the flour into a large bowl. Rub the butter into the flour with your fingertips until it resembles fine breadcrumbs. Make a well in the centre and add the egg and 1–2 tablespoons water and mix with a flat-bladed knife, using a cutting action, until the mixture comes together in beads.

3 Gently gather the dough together and lift out onto a lightly floured work surface. Press together into a ball, wrap in plastic wrap and refrigerate for 30 minutes.

4 Preheat the oven to moderately hot 200°C (400°F/Gas 6). Grease four 9 cm pie tins. Divide the dough into four pieces. Roll each piece of dough out between two sheets of baking paper to a 20 cm circle. Press the pastry into the tins, leaving the excess overhanging.

5 Divide the filling among the tins. Fold over the excess pastry, pleating as you go. Place on a baking tray and bake for 20–25 minutes, or until the pastry is golden. Combine the preserved lemon and yoghurt and serve with the pies.

NUTRITION PER SERVE
Protein 40 g; Fat 40 g; Carbohydrate 64 g; Dietary Fibre 6.5 g; Cholesterol 205 mg; 3183 kJ (760 cal)

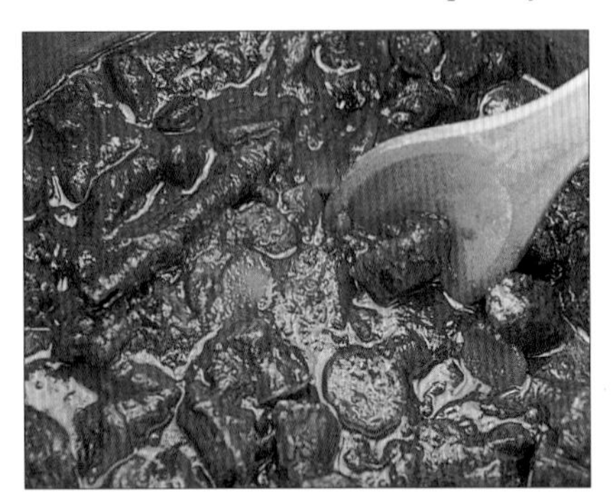

Cook the beef mixture until the liquid has reduced and thickened slightly.

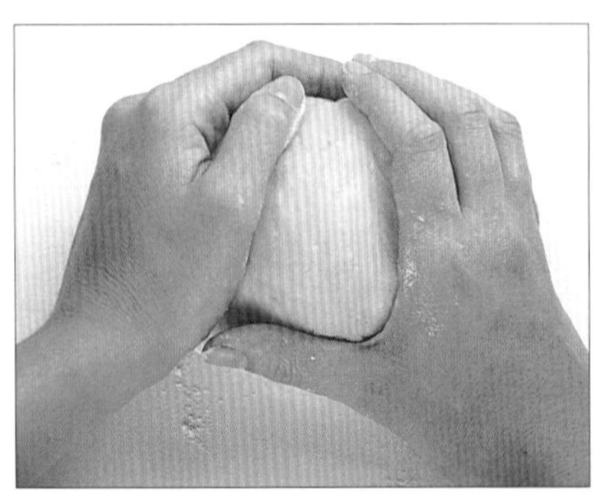

Gently gather the dough together and press into a ball.

Fold the excess pastry in pleats over the filling.

PASTA WITH BABY SPINACH, ROASTED PUMPKIN & TOMATO

Preparation time: 15 minutes
Total cooking time: 1 hour
Serves 4

750 g sweet pumpkin (e.g. butternut or jap)
2 tablespoons Parmesan-infused olive oil (see Note)
16 unpeeled cloves garlic
250 g cherry tomatoes, halved
500 g orecchiette or penne
200 g baby English spinach leaves
200 g marinated Persian feta (see Note)
1/4 cup (60 ml) sherry vinegar
2 tablespoons walnut oil

1 Preheat the oven to moderately hot 200°C (400°F/Gas 6). Cut the pumpkin into large cubes, place in a roasting tin and drizzle with Parmesan oil. Roast for 30 minutes, then add the garlic. Arrange the tomatoes on a baking tray. Put all the vegetables in the oven and roast for 10–15 minutes, or until cooked. Don't overcook the tomatoes or they will turn to mush.
2 Cook the pasta according to the packet instructions until *al dente*. Drain well.
3 Toss together the pasta, tomatoes, pumpkin, garlic and spinach in a large bowl.
4 Drain the feta and reserve 1/4 cup (60 ml) marinade. Whisk together the reserved marinade, vinegar and walnut oil. Pour over the pasta and sprinkle with pieces of the cheese.

NUTRITION PER SERVE
Protein 29 g; Fat 34 g; Carbohydrate 105 g; Dietary Fibre 13 g; Cholesterol 34 mg; 3524 kJ (842 cal)

COOK'S FILE

NOTES: Parmesan-infused olive oil is available at gourmet food stores and really adds depth of flavour.

Persian feta is softer and creamier than other feta and is marinated in oil, herbs and garlic.

Help your guests by peeling the garlic after roasting it.

VARIATION: Toss in 200 g marinated Kalamata olives for added flavour.

Drizzle the cubes of pumpkin with Parmesan-infused olive oil.

Roast the pumpkin, garlic and tomatoes until they are cooked.

Cook the pasta in a large saucepan of boiling water until al dente.

LAMB SHANKS WITH PUY LENTILS

Preparation time: 25 minutes
Total cooking time: 1 hour 45 minutes
Serves 4

1/3 cup (80 ml) olive oil
4 French-trimmed lamb shanks (280 g each) (see Note)
6 cloves garlic, unpeeled
1 onion, thinly sliced
1 red capsicum, sliced
2 cloves garlic, crushed
400 g can peeled tomatoes, chopped
1 cup (250 ml) white wine
1 bay leaf
1 cinnamon stick
2 strips orange rind
1 1/2 cups (320 g) puy lentils
400 g can cannellini beans, rinsed and drained
2 spring onions, sliced
pinch saffron threads
1 teaspoon ground coriander
1 teaspoon ground cumin
3 tablespoons chopped fresh flat-leaf parsley

1 Preheat the oven to moderately hot 200°C (400°F/Gas 6). Heat half the oil in a large deep ovenproof casserole dish, add the shanks in batches and cook over medium heat for 4 minutes, or until the shanks are brown on all sides. Remove from the dish.
2 Place the unpeeled garlic cloves on a baking tray and drizzle with half the remaining oil.
3 Add the onion, capsicum and crushed garlic to the ovenproof dish and cook until golden. Stir in the tomato, wine, bay leaf, cinnamon stick and orange rind, return all the shanks, then cover and transfer to the oven. Cook for 1 hour, then uncover and cook for a further 30 minutes, or until the shanks are tender and the meat is just falling off the bone. Keep warm. Add the tray with the garlic cloves to the oven 15 minutes before the shanks will be ready and cook until they are soft. Cool slightly, then peel.
4 Meanwhile, place the lentils in a saucepan, cover with 1.5 litres water and bring to the boil. Cook over high heat for 20 minutes, or until tender. Drain, reserving the cooking liquid.
5 Place the garlic in a food processor with the cannellini beans and a little of the reserved lentil cooking liquid and process until smooth and creamy, then season to taste with salt and cracked black pepper. Cover and keep warm. Add more of the cooking liquid if it starts to thicken and dry out.
6 Heat the remaining oil in a large frying pan, add the spring onion and spices and cook over medium heat for 3 minutes, or until fragrant. Stir in the lentils and parsley and cook until warmed through.
7 To serve, place a mound of lentils on each plate, stand the shanks upright in the lentils and drizzle with some of the cooking liquid from the shanks. Serve a spoonful of the bean purée on the side.

NUTRITION PER SERVE
Protein 70 g; Fat 35 g; Carbohydrate 45 g; Dietary Fibre 2 g; Cholesterol 130 mg; 3437 kJ (820 cal)

COOK'S FILE

NOTE: French-trimmed lamb shanks are lamb shanks that have the meat scraped back to make a neat lamb 'drumstick'. The bone is usually cut shorter than normal. You can use normal lamb shanks instead.

Cook the lamb shanks in batches until brown all over.

Add the onion, capsicum and garlic to the dish and cook until golden.

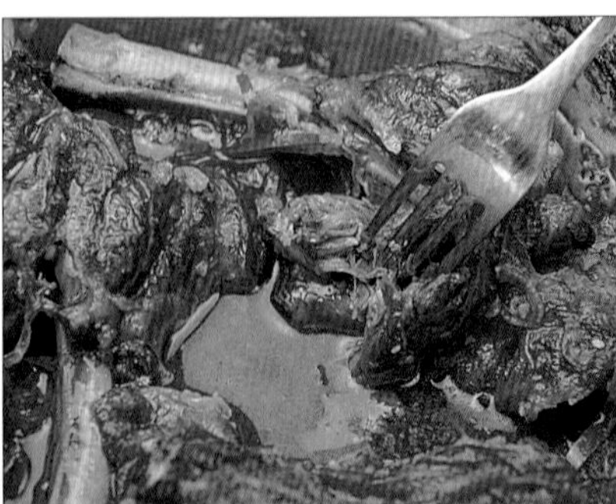

Cook the lamb shanks until the meat is just falling off the bone.

When the garlic is cool enough to handle, peel off the skin.

Cover the the puy lentils with water and cook until they are tender.

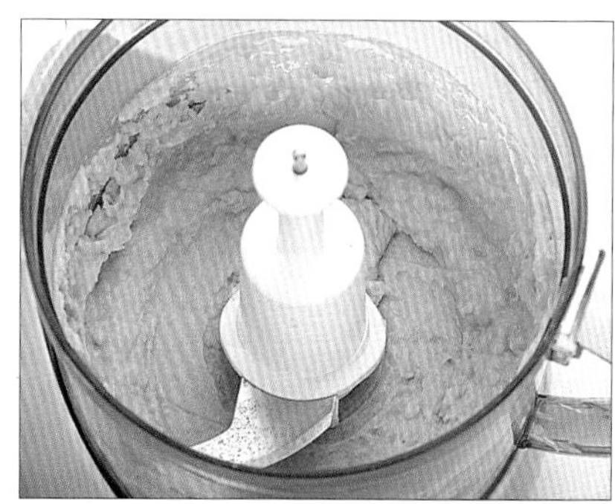

Process the cannellini bean mixture until smooth and creamy.

TUNA STEAKS ON CORIANDER NOODLES

Preparation time: 15 minutes
Total cooking time: 10 minutes
Serves 4

1/4 cup (60 ml) lime juice
2 tablespoons fish sauce
2 tablespoons sweet chilli sauce
2 teaspoons grated palm sugar
1 teaspoon sesame oil
1 clove garlic, finely chopped
1 tablespoon virgin olive oil
4 tuna steaks (150 g each), at room temperature
200 g dried thin wheat noodles
6 spring onions, thinly sliced
3/4 cup (25 g) chopped fresh coriander leaves
lime wedges, to garnish

1 To make the dressing, place the lime juice, fish sauce, chilli sauce, sugar, sesame oil and garlic in a small bowl and mix together.

2 Heat the olive oil in a chargrill pan. Add the tuna steaks and cook over high heat for 2 minutes each side, or until cooked to your liking. Transfer the steaks to a warm plate, cover and keep warm.

3 Place the noodles in a large saucepan of lightly salted, rapidly boiling water and return to the boil. Cook for 4 minutes, or until the noodles are tender. Drain well. Add half the dressing and half the spring onion and coriander to the noodles and gently toss together.

4 Either cut the tuna into even cubes or slice it.

5 Place the noodles on serving plates and top with the tuna. Mix the remaining dressing with the spring onion and coriander and drizzle over the tuna. Garnish with lime wedges.

NUTRITION PER SERVE
Protein 32 g; Fat 10 g; Carbohydrate 5 g; Dietary Fibre 1 g; Cholesterol 105 mg; 1030 kJ (245 cal)

COOK'S FILE

NOTE: If you prefer, you can serve the tuna steaks whole rather than cutting them into cubes. If serving whole, they would look better served with the noodles on the side.

Cook the tuna steaks in a chargrill pan until cooked to your liking.

Cook the noodles in lightly salted water until tender.

Combine the remaining dressing with the spring onion and coriander.

STEAMED LEMON GRASS AND GINGER CHICKEN WITH ASIAN GREENS

Preparation time: 25 minutes
Total cooking time: 40 minutes
Serves 4

200 g fresh egg noodles
4 chicken breast fillets
2 stems lemon grass
5 cm piece fresh ginger, cut into julienne strips
1 lime, thinly sliced
2 cups (500 ml) chicken stock
1 bunch (350 g) choy sum, cut into 10 cm lengths
800 g Chinese broccoli, cut into 10 cm lengths
1/4 cup (60 ml) kecap manis
1/4 cup (60 ml) soy sauce
1 teaspoon sesame oil
toasted sesame seeds, to garnish

1 Cook the egg noodles in a saucepan of boiling water for 5 minutes, then drain and keep warm.
2 Cut each chicken breast fillet horizontally through the middle so that you are left with eight thin flat chicken fillets.
3 Cut the lemon grass into lengths that are about 5 cm longer than the chicken fillets, then cut in half lengthways. Place one piece of lemon grass onto one half of each chicken breast fillet, top with some ginger and lime slices, then top with the other half of the fillet.
4 Pour the stock into a wok and bring to a simmer. Place two of the chicken fillets in a paper-lined bamboo steamer. Place the steamer over the wok and steam over the simmering stock for 12–15 minutes, or until the chicken is tender. Remove the chicken from the steamer, cover and keep warm. Repeat with the other fillets.
5 Steam the greens in the same way for 3 minutes, or until tender. Bring the stock in the wok to the boil.
6 Place the kecap manis, soy sauce and sesame oil in a bowl and whisk together well.
7 Divide the noodles among four serving plates and ladle the boiling stock over them. Top with a neat pile of Asian greens, then add the chicken and generously drizzle each serve with the sauce. Sprinkle with toasted sesame seeds and serve.

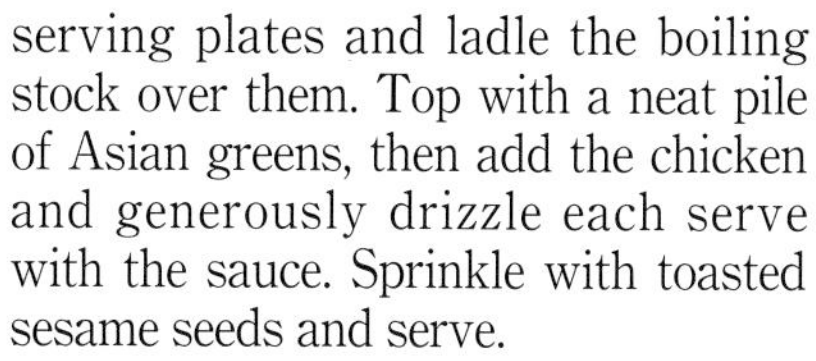

NUTRITION PER SERVE
Protein 65 g; Fat 7.5 g; Carbohydrate 37 g; Dietary Fibre 9 g; Cholesterol 119 mg; 2045 kJ (488 cal)

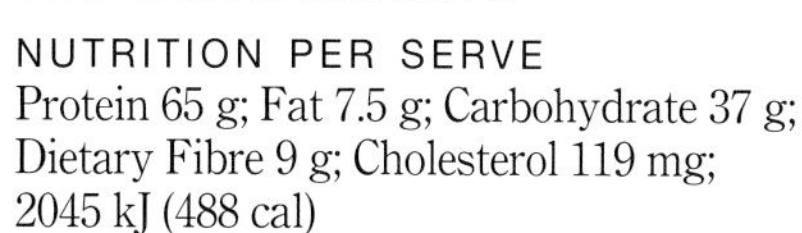

Cut each chicken breast in half horizontally through the middle.

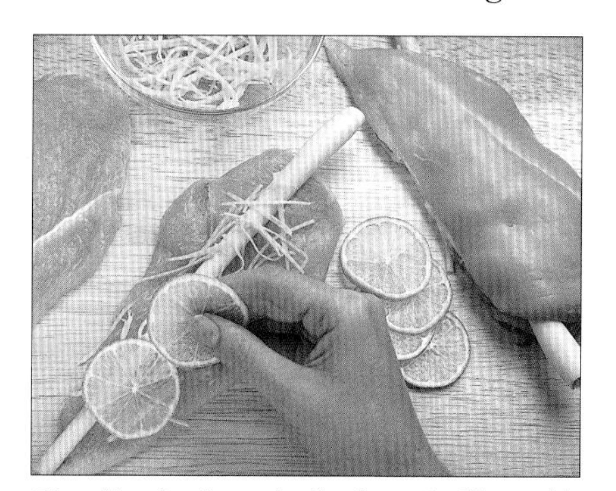

Top the bottom half of each fillet with lemon grass, ginger and lime.

Steam the lemon grass chicken fillets until cooked and tender.

MEDITERRANEAN BURGERS

Preparation time: 15 minutes
Total cooking time: 20 minutes
Serves 4

1 large red capsicum
500 g lamb mince
1 egg, lightly beaten
1 small onion, grated
3 cloves garlic, crushed
2 tablespoons pine nuts, chopped
1 tablespoon finely chopped fresh mint
1 tablespoon finely chopped fresh parsley
1 teaspoon ground cumin
2 teaspoons chilli sauce
1 tablespoon olive oil
4 Turkish or pide bread rolls
1 cup (220 g) ready-made hummus
100 g baby rocket
1 small Lebanese cucumber, cut into ribbons
chilli sauce, to serve (optional)

1 Cut the capsicum into large pieces, removing the seeds and membrane. Place, skin-side-up, under a hot grill until the skin blackens and blisters. Cool in a plastic bag, then peel and cut into thick strips.
2 Combine the mince, egg, onion, garlic, pine nuts, fresh herbs, cumin and chilli sauce in a large bowl. Mix with your hands and roll into four even-sized balls. Press the balls into large patties about 9 cm in diameter.
3 Heat the oil in a large frying pan and cook the patties over medium heat for 6 minutes each side, or until well browned and cooked through, then drain on paper towels.
4 Halve the rolls and toast both sides.
5 Spread the cut sides of the rolls with hummus, then lay rocket leaves, roasted capsicum and cucumber ribbons over the base. Place a patty on the salad and top with the other half of the roll. Serve with chilli sauce.

NUTRITION PER SERVE
Protein 40 g; Fat 30 g; Carbohydrate 54 g; Dietary Fibre 7 g; Cholesterol 124 mg; 2758 kJ (660 cal)

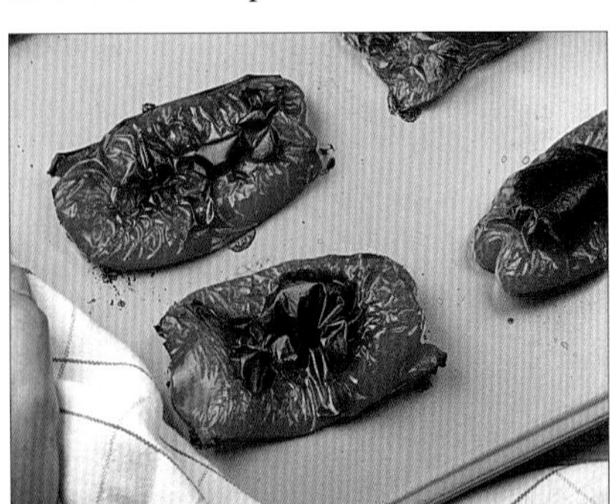

Cook the capsicum under a hot grill until the skin blackens and blisters.

Roll the mince mixture into even-sized balls and then flatten into patties.

SATAY CHICKEN BURGERS

Preparation time: 1 hour
Total cooking time: 35 minutes
Serves 4

Satay sauce
1 1/2 bird's-eye chillies, chopped
2 cm x 1 cm piece ginger, chopped
2 cloves garlic, peeled
2 tablespoons chopped red Asian shallots
2 fresh coriander roots
1 tablespoon peanut oil
1/4 cup (60 g) smooth peanut butter
200 ml coconut milk
1 tablespoon lime juice
1 teaspoon soft brown sugar
2 teaspoons fish sauce
2 teaspoons soy sauce

Cucumber relish
1/2 small red onion, thinly sliced
1 small red chilli, seeded and thinly sliced
2 tablespoons rice vinegar
1 tablespoon sugar
1 clove garlic, crushed
1 tablespoon fish sauce
1 telegraph cucumber, cut into ribbons

Burgers
500 g chicken mince
1/4 cup (30 g) finely chopped spring onions
4 tablespoons finely chopped fresh coriander leaves
2 cloves garlic, crushed
1/4 teaspoon cayenne pepper
1 teaspoon finely chopped lime rind
2 teaspoons finely chopped fresh ginger
2 tablespoons vegetable oil
4 soft flat bread rolls, halved

1 To make the satay sauce, grind together the chilli, ginger, garlic, shallots and coriander roots in a food processor or mortar and pestle to make a paste. If necessary, add a little water. Heat the peanut oil in a saucepan over medium heat, add the paste and cook for about 3 minutes, or until soft and fragrant. Whisk in the peanut butter and coconut milk and bring to the boil. Reduce the heat and simmer for 7 minutes, or until thick. Add the remaining ingredients and simmer for 4 minutes, or until the oil starts to separate and the mixture thickens. Whisk, then remove from the heat and cool.

2 To make the relish, place all the ingredients and 1 teaspoon salt in a bowl and toss together.

3 Preheat the oven to warm 170°C (325°F/Gas 3). Combine the mince, spring onion, coriander, garlic, cayenne pepper, lime and ginger. Shape into four patties. Heat the oil in a large frying pan over medium heat. Cook the patties for 4 minutes each side, or until browned. Transfer to a baking tray and bake for 8 minutes, or until cooked through. Serve on rolls with the satay sauce and cucumber relish.

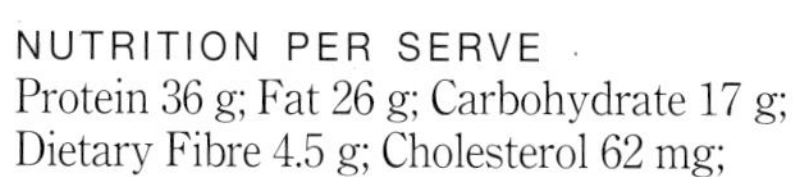

NUTRITION PER SERVE
Protein 36 g; Fat 26 g; Carbohydrate 17 g; Dietary Fibre 4.5 g; Cholesterol 62 mg; 1842 kJ (440 cal)

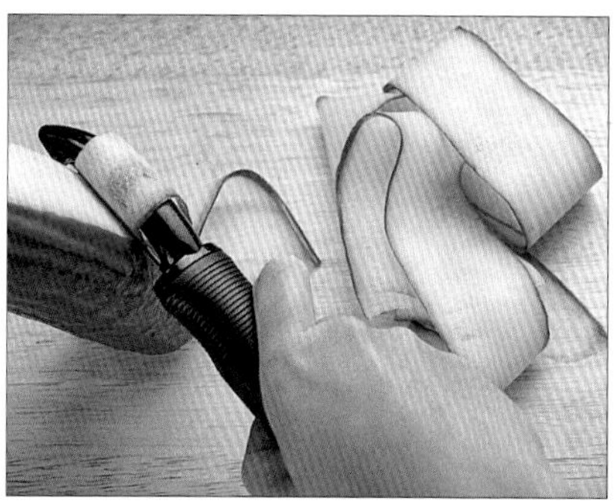

Using a vegetable peeler, cut the cucumber into thin ribbons.

Simmer the sauce until the oil starts to separate and the mixture thickens.

LAMB BACKSTRAPS WITH SPICY LENTILS AND RAITA

Preparation time: 30 minutes + 30 minutes standing
Total cooking time: 1 hour
Serves 4

Spicy lentils
2 tablespoons olive oil
1 onion, chopped
1 carrot, diced
3 cloves garlic, finely chopped
2 teaspoons ground coriander
1/2 teaspoon ground cinnamon
1/2 teaspoon ground cloves
1 teaspoon ground turmeric
2 teaspoons ground cumin
1/2 teaspoon cayenne pepper
1 large tomato, diced
1 cup (185 g) brown lentils, washed
chopped fresh coriander, to garnish

Raita
1 Lebanese cucumber, deseeded and grated
1 cup (250 g) plain yoghurt
1/2 small red onion, finely chopped
1 clove garlic, crushed
3 tablespoons fresh coriander leaves, chopped
1 tablespoon lemon juice
1/2 teaspoon ground cumin
pinch cayenne pepper

Lamb
2.5 cm cinnamon stick
2 teaspoons cardamom seeds
2 cloves
2 teaspoons cumin seeds
1/2 teaspoon chilli flakes
1 tablespoon coriander seeds
two 25 cm lamb backstraps or loin fillets (250 g each)
1 tablespoon olive oil

1 To make the spicy lentils, heat the oil in a large saucepan, add the onion and carrot and cook, stirring, for 7 minutes, or until the onion is soft. Stir in the garlic and cook for 2–3 minutes, then add the spices and stir for 1 minute, or until fragrant. Add the tomato, lentils, 1 teaspoon salt and 1 litre water. Bring to the boil, then reduce the heat and simmer for 30–40 minutes, or until the lentils are soft and most of the liquid is absorbed. Add more water if it is too dry. Season.

2 Meanwhile, to prepare the raita, toss the cucumber with 1 teaspoon salt and drain in a colander for 30 minutes. Rinse, then squeeze the cucumber to remove any excess liquid and combine with the remaining ingredients. Leave until ready to use.

3 Preheat the oven to very hot 240°C (475°F/Gas 9). Preheat a baking tray. Combine the spices for the lamb in a dry frying pan and toast, shaking the pan frequently, over medium heat for 2 minutes, or until smoking and fragrant. Grind the spices together coarsely. Season the lamb, then rub on the spice blend.

4 Heat a large frying pan over medium heat. Add the oil, then the lamb and brown each side for 2 minutes. Transfer to the hot baking tray and roast for 3–5 minutes, or until cooked to your liking. Remove from the oven, cover with foil and rest for 5–10 minutes. Cut the meat across the grain into 1 cm slices.

5 Place a mound of lentils in the centre of each plate. Arrange 6–8 lamb pieces around the lentils, then add a dollop of raita. Garnish with coriander.

NUTRITION PER SERVE
Protein 43 g; Fat 22 g; Carbohydrate 24 g; Dietary Fibre 9 g; Cholesterol 92 mg; 1975 kJ (472 cal)

Cook the onion and carrot until the onion has softened.

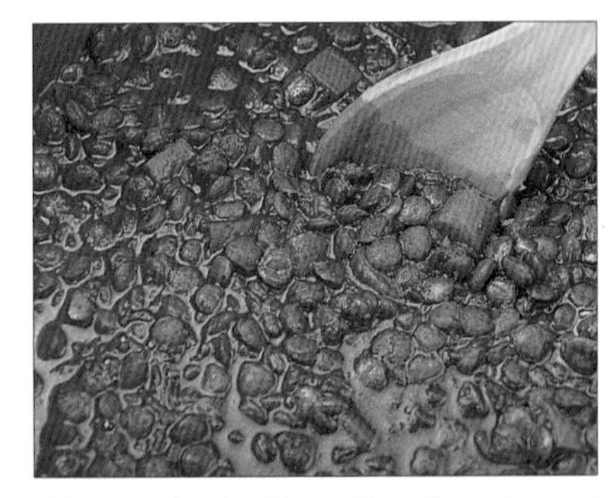

Simmer the lentils until soft and most of the liquid has been absorbed.

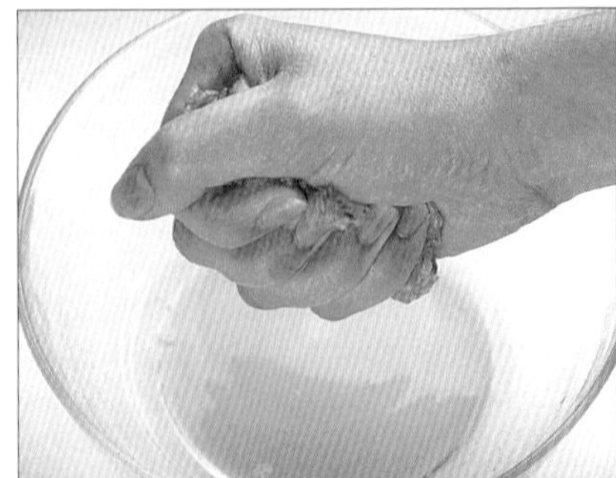

Squeeze the cucumber to remove any excess liquid.

Toast the spices in a dry frying pan until fragrant.

Rub the spice blend on the seasoned lamb backstraps.

Cook the lamb backstraps until browned on both sides.

ROASTED PORK WITH RICE NOODLE CAKE AND CUCUMBER SALAD

Preparation time: 40 minutes + 5 minutes soaking
Total cooking time: 25 minutes
Serves 4

500 g thin fresh rice noodles, at room temperature
2 Lebanese cucumbers, halved lengthways and thinly sliced
2 tablespoons chopped fresh coriander leaves
1 tablespoon lime juice
1 tablespoon fish sauce
2 teaspoons caster sugar
1/4 cup (60 ml) oil
1 red capsicum, thinly sliced
3 cloves garlic, finely chopped
1 tablespoon white vinegar
1/4 cup (60 ml) black bean sauce
1/3 cup (80 ml) chicken stock
1 tablespoon soft brown sugar
300 g Chinese roasted pork, sliced

1 Pour boiling water over the noodles and leave for 5 minutes, or until softened. Drain, then separate by pulling apart slightly.

2 To make the cucumber salad, toss the cucumber, coriander, lime juice, fish sauce and caster sugar together in a large bowl and leave until needed.

3 Heat 1 tablespoon of the oil in a large non-stick frying pan. Place four 9.5 cm (2.5 cm deep) rings in the frying pan. Fill as firmly as possible with the noodles and press down with the back of a spoon. Cook over medium heat for 10 minutes, or until crisp, pressing the noodles down occasionally. Turn over and repeat on the other side, adding another tablespoon of the oil if necessary. Cover and keep warm.

4 Meanwhile, heat 1 tablespoon of the remaining oil in a wok, add the capsicum and stir-fry over high heat for 2 minutes, or until the capsicum has softened slightly. Add the garlic to the wok and toss for 1 minute, or until softened, then add the vinegar, black bean sauce, stock and sugar. Stir until the sugar has dissolved, then simmer for 2 minutes, or until the sauce thickens slightly. Add the Chinese roasted pork and stir to coat with the sauce.

5 To serve, place a noodle cake on each plate and top with some of the roasted pork mixture. Arrange the salad around the noodle cake and serve.

NUTRITION PER SERVE
Protein 34 g; Fat 28 g; Carbohydrate 100 g; Dietary Fibre 7 g; Cholesterol 70 mg; 3360 kJ (805 cal)

Soak the noodles in boiling water until they are soft.

Press the noodles down into the rings with the back of a spoon.

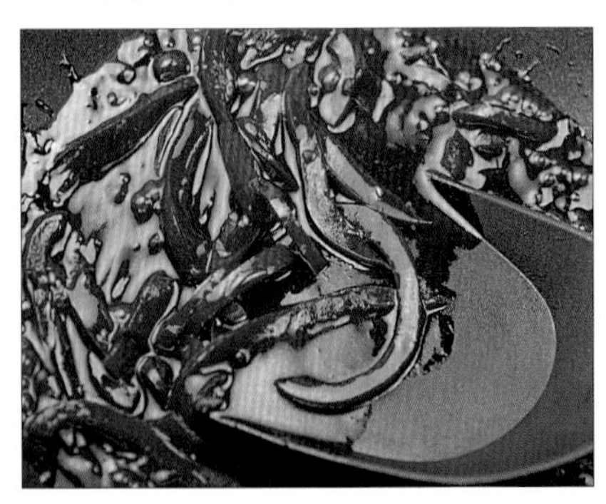

Simmer until the sugar dissolves and the sauce slightly thickens.

SALMON WITH ASIAN GREENS AND CHILLI JAM

Preparation time: 20 minutes
Total cooking time: 1 hour
Serves 4

- 1 tablespoon peanut oil
- 1 red capsicum, thinly sliced
- 500 g baby bok choy, quartered
- 1 clove garlic, finely chopped
- 1 tablespoon soy sauce
- 1 teaspoon sugar
- 1 tablespoon vegetable oil, for pan-frying, extra
- 4 salmon cutlets (150–200 g each)

Chilli jam

- 2 1/2 tablespoons vegetable oil
- 1 large onion, thinly sliced
- 6 red bird's-eye chillies, seeded and thinly sliced
- 2 teaspoons grated fresh ginger
- 3/4 cup (185 ml) white wine vinegar
- 3/4 cup (140 g) soft brown sugar
- 2 teaspoons lime juice

1 To make the chilli jam, heat the oil in a saucepan and add the onion, chilli and ginger. Cook over medium heat for 3–4 minutes, or until the onion is soft. Add the remaining ingredients and 1/4 cup (60 ml) water and stir until the sugar dissolves. Bring to the boil, then reduce the heat and simmer for 35–40 minutes, or until thick and pulpy (it will thicken as it cools). Cool slightly, transfer to a food processor, then process until smooth. Cool.

2 Heat the peanut oil in a frying pan, add the capsicum and cook over medium heat for 2 minutes, or until softened slightly, then add the bok choy and cook for 1 minute, or until wilted. Add the garlic and cook until fragrant. Reduce the heat, add the soy sauce and sugar and warm gently. Remove from the heat and keep warm.

3 Heat the extra oil in a frying pan, season the salmon and cook over medium heat for 2 minutes each side, or until cooked to your liking. It should be just rare in the centre—do not overcook or the flesh will dry out.

4 Divide the vegetables among four plates and top with a salmon cutlet. Dollop with chilli jam and serve.

NUTRITION PER SERVE

Protein 50 g; Fat 27 g; Carbohydrate 40 g; Dietary Fibre 6.5 g; Cholesterol 140 mg; 2513 kJ (600 cal)

Simmer the jam until it thickens and becomes pulpy.

Cook the seasoned salmon cutlets until done to your liking.

PROSCIUTTO-WRAPPED PORK WITH POLENTA

Preparation time: 25 minutes + 10 minutes resting
Total cooking time: 40 minutes
Serves 4

8 slices prosciutto
4 thin pork fillets (200 g each)
24 large sage leaves
2 tablespoons olive oil
1 cup (250 ml) verjuice or white wine
2 tablespoons balsamic vinegar
200 g cherry tomatoes
20 g butter, melted
1 litre chicken stock
1 cup (170 g) fine instant polenta
50 g butter, extra
100 g mascarpone
1/2 cup (45 g) grated pecorino cheese

1 Preheat the oven to moderately hot 200°C (400°F/Gas 6). Wrap two slices of prosciutto around each pork fillet, tucking in three sage leaves as you go. Secure with toothpicks.
2 Heat the oil in a frying pan over high heat and cook the pork in batches for 3 minutes, or until golden, then transfer to a baking dish. Deglaze the pan by adding the verjuice and vinegar and scraping up any sediment. Pour the pan juices over the pork, bake for 10 minutes, then cover and rest for 10 minutes. (Leave the oven on.)
3 Lay out the tomatoes in a roasting tin and roast for 10 minutes, or until tender. Keep the tomatoes warm.
4 Meanwhile, brush both sides of the remaining sage leaves with the melted butter, lay on a baking tray and bake for 5 minutes, or until crisp.
5 Bring the stock to the boil in a large saucepan, then slowly add the polenta, stirring constantly. Cook, stirring, for 8–10 minutes, or until smooth and thick. Stir in the butter, mascarpone and pecorino and season.
6 Lay slices of pork on a bed of polenta, drizzle with the cooking juices and top with the tomatoes. Scatter with the sage leaves and serve.

NUTRITION PER SERVE
Protein 40 g; Fat 34 g; Carbohydrate 7 g; Dietary Fibre 1 g; Cholesterol 142 mg; 2235 kJ (535 cal)

Secure the prosciutto and sage leaves with toothpicks.

Stir the liquid, scraping any sediment from the bottom of the pan.

Roast the tomatoes in a roasting tin until tender.

Cook the polenta, stirring constantly, until smooth and thick.

BLUE-EYE WITH SALSA VERDE POTATOES

Preparation time: 20 minutes
Total cooking time: 25 minutes
Serves 4

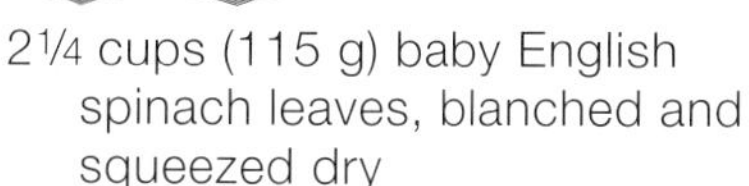

2 1/4 cups (115 g) baby English spinach leaves, blanched and squeezed dry
2 tablespoons chopped fresh flat-leaf parsley
2 tablespoons snipped fresh chives
1 tablespoon drained capers
2 anchovy fillets
1 hard-boiled egg, chopped
1 tablespoon white wine vinegar
1/4 cup (60 ml) extra virgin olive oil
500 g pink eye or desirée potatoes
2 tablespoons vegetable oil
4 blue-eye or other firm white fish fillets (150 g each)
125 g butter
3 cloves garlic, finely chopped
1 tablespoon lime juice
1 1/2 tablespoons lime zest

1 To make the salsa verde, place the spinach, parsley, chives, capers, anchovy fillets, egg and vinegar in a food processor and process until combined. With the motor running, gradually add the extra virgin olive oil in a thin, steady stream and process until smooth.
2 Cook the potatoes in a large saucepan of boiling water for about 18 minutes, or until tender. Drain and cool slightly, then cut into 1 cm slices. Carefully fold the salsa verde through the warm potatoes.
3 Meanwhile, heat the vegetable oil in a frying pan over medium heat and cook the fish in batches for 3–5 minutes each side, or until tender. Remove from the pan and keep warm.
4 Reduce the heat slightly, add the butter and cook until just brown, then stir in the garlic and lime juice.
5 Serve the blue-eye on a bed of potatoes, then drizzle with the butter and top with lime zest.

NUTRITION PER SERVE
Protein 37 g; Fat 55 g; Carbohydrate 22 g; Dietary Fibre 3.5 g; Cholesterol 240 mg; 3052 kJ (730 cal)

Add the oil in a thin stream and process until smooth.

Cook the fish in batches until tender and lightly browned.

Cook the butter until it browns, then add the garlic and lime juice.

CHICKEN WITH CORIANDER CHUTNEY AND SPICED EGGPLANT

Preparation time: 1 hour 10 minutes + overnight refrigeration + 30 minutes soaking
Total cooking time: 1 hour 10 minutes
Serves 4

1 cup (250 g) plain yoghurt
1 tablespoon lemon juice
1/2 onion, coarsely chopped
2 cloves garlic, finely chopped
2 teaspoons finely chopped fresh ginger
1/2 teaspoon ground cumin
750 g chicken thighs, trimmed of fat, cut into 4 cm cubes
4 pieces ready-made naan
plain yoghurt, to serve

Spiced eggplant
1 large eggplant
2 tablespoons oil
1 onion, finely chopped
3 teaspoons finely chopped fresh ginger
2 cloves garlic, crushed
1/2 teaspoon ground turmeric
1 teaspoon ground cumin
1 tomato, finely diced
2 teaspoons lemon juice

Coriander chutney
1/4 cup (60 ml) lemon juice
2 cups (100 g) coarsely chopped fresh coriander leaves and stems
1/4 cup (35 g) finely chopped onion
1 tablespoon finely chopped fresh ginger
1/2 jalapeño pepper, seeded and finely chopped
1 teaspoon sugar

1 Combine the yoghurt, lemon, onion, garlic, ginger and cumin in a large non-metallic bowl, add the chicken and toss. Cover and refrigerate overnight.
2 Preheat the oven to very hot 240°C (475°F/Gas 9). Soak eight wooden skewers in water for 30 minutes. To make the purée, prick the eggplant in a few places, put on a baking tray and bake for 35–40 minutes, or until soft and wrinkled. Cool. Reduce the oven to moderately hot 200°C (400°F/Gas 6).
3 Meanwhile, to make the chutney, put the lemon juice, coriander and 1/4 cup (60 ml) water in a food processor and process until smooth. Add the remaining ingredients and season.
4 When the eggplant is cool enough to handle, cut in half, scoop out the flesh and coarsely chop. Heat the oil in a frying pan over medium heat. Add the onion and cook for 5 minutes, or until soft. Add the ginger and garlic and cook for 2 minutes, or until fragrant. Add the spices and cook for 1 minute, then add the tomato and 1/4 cup (60 ml) water and simmer for 5 minutes, or until the tomato is soft and the mixture is thick. Stir in the eggplant and lemon juice and season. Cook for 2 more minutes, then remove from the heat and keep warm.
5 Thread the chicken onto skewers and chargrill over medium heat for 4–6 minutes each side, or until tender.
6 Meanwhile, heat the naan in the oven for 5 minutes. Reheat the eggplant over low heat if needed. Place the naan on a plate and spread a quarter of the eggplant in the centre, leaving a 4 cm border. Lay two chicken skewers on top and drizzle with chutney and yoghurt.

NUTRITION PER SERVE
Protein 50 g; Fat 17 g; Carbohydrate 26 g; Dietary Fibre 5.5 g; Cholesterol 105 mg; 1956 kJ (467 cal)

Combine the marinade ingredients in a bowl and toss the chicken in it.

Roast the eggplant on a baking tray until very soft and wrinkled.

Process the coriander, lemon juice and water until smooth.

Cut the eggplant in half, scoop out the flesh and coarsely chop.

Simmer until the tomato has softened and the mixture has thickened.

Chargrill the chicken skewers until cooked through but still tender.

LEMON CHICKEN ON BASIL MASH WITH GARLIC LEMON AIOLI

Preparation time: 20 minutes + overnight refrigeration
Total cooking time: 25 minutes
Serves 4

1/4 cup (60 ml) lemon juice
2 cloves garlic, crushed
1/3 cup (80 ml) olive oil
4 corn-fed chicken breast fillets (150 g each), skin on
1/3 cup (90 g) whole-egg mayonnaise
1 tablespoon lemon juice, extra
2 cloves garlic, crushed, extra
800 g desirée potatoes, cut into large chunks
1 1/2 tablespoons butter
1/3 cup (90 g) sour cream
1 teaspoon sea salt flakes
2 tablespoons finely shredded fresh basil

1 Combine the lemon juice, garlic and half the oil in a non-metallic flat dish. Coat the chicken in the marinade, then cover with plastic wrap and refrigerate overnight.

2 To make the aïoli, combine the mayonnaise, extra lemon juice and half the extra garlic in a small bowl, then season to taste. Cover.

3 Cook the potato in a saucepan of boiling water for 12 minutes, or until soft. Drain, then return to the heat until all the moisture has been absorbed. Add the butter, sour cream, sea salt and remaining garlic and mash with a potato masher until smooth and lump free. Remove from the heat and cover.

4 Meanwhile, drain the chicken. Heat the remaining oil in a large frying pan over medium heat until sizzling. Add the chicken breasts, skin-side-down, and cook for 4–5 minutes, or until the skin is golden and crispy, then turn and cook for 5 minutes, or until tender and cooked through. Rest for 5 minutes.

5 Stir the shredded basil through the mash just before serving.

6 To serve, put a dollop of mash on the centre of each plate, top with a chicken breast, then some aïoli. Season and serve with a crisp green salad.

NUTRITION PER SERVE
Protein 40 g; Fat 45 g; Carbohydrate 32 g; Dietary Fibre 4 g; Cholesterol 130 mg; 2892 kJ (690 cal)

Mash the potato with a potato masher until smooth and free of lumps.

Cook the chicken until the skin is crisp and golden.

TAPENADE-COATED LAMB RACKS WITH FETA AND COUSCOUS

Preparation time: 30 minutes + 15 minutes standing
Total cooking time: 1 hour 10 minutes
Serves 4

2 teaspoons capers
15 g drained anchovy fillets
1 clove garlic
3/4 cup (90 g) sliced pitted black olives
1 1/2 tablespoons lemon juice
1 1/2 tablespoons extra virgin olive oil
1 tablespoon cognac
8 small ripe Roma tomatoes, halved
150 g Bulgarian feta (see Note)
4 lamb racks with 3 cutlets each
1 1/2 cups (375 ml) chicken stock
1 tablespoon olive oil
1 red onion, thinly sliced
1 tablespoon baby capers
1 cup (185 g) couscous
1 teaspoon orange zest
25 g butter
1 1/2 tablespoons chopped fresh mint

1 Preheat the oven to moderate 180°C (350°F/Gas 4). To make the tapenade, put the capers, anchovy fillets, garlic, olives and lemon juice in a food processor or blender and process until finely chopped. While the motor is running, slowly pour in the extra virgin olive oil and cognac. Season with pepper.

2 Place the tomatoes on a wire rack in a roasting tin, sprinkle with salt and pepper and roast for 40 minutes, or until slightly dried. Sprinkle with the crumbled feta. Increase the oven to hot 220°C (425°F/Gas 7).

3 Trim and clean the lamb racks, then coat them in the tapenade and place in a roasting tin. Cook for 20–25 minutes, or until cooked to your liking. Rest for 10 minutes before carving into cutlets.

4 Bring the chicken stock to the boil in a saucepan. Meanwhile, heat the olive oil in a frying pan, add the onion and baby capers and cook over medium heat for 5 minutes, or until the onion is tender. Transfer to a bowl, add the couscous, orange zest and butter and cover with the boiling stock. Leave for 5 minutes, or until all the liquid has been absorbed. Fluff with a fork to separate the grains, adding half the mint.

5 To serve, place a mound of couscous in the centre of four serving plates. Top with a cutlet, then a piece of tomato, another cutlet, another tomato half and finish with a cutlet. Lean two pieces of tomato up against the side of each stack, sprinkle with the remaining mint and serve.

NUTRITION PER SERVE
Protein 38 g; Fat 30 g; Carbohydrate 36 g; Dietary Fibre 3.5 g; Cholesterol 124 mg; 2394 kJ (572 cal)

COOK'S FILE

NOTE: Bulgarian feta has a distinctive flavour, but you can use normal feta.
HINT: To save time, use 1/2 cup (155 g) good-quality bought olive tapenade.

Bake the tomatoes on a wire rack until they are slightly dried.

Trim the fat from the lamb racks and clean the bones.

BEEF FILLET WITH ROASTED TOMATO BEARNAISE

Preparation time: 35 minutes + 30 minutes standing
Total cooking time: 2 hours 15 minutes
Serves 4

- 6 Roma tomatoes
- 1/2 teaspoon sugar
- 1/3 cup (80 ml) olive oil
- 1 1/2 teaspoons sea salt flakes
- 1/4 cup (60 ml) tarragon vinegar
- 4 black peppercorns
- 1/2 cup (125 ml) dry white wine
- 3 French shallots, chopped
- 1 large Pontiac potato
- 1 large orange sweet potato
- 1 large parsnip
- 1 celeriac
- 4 fillet steaks (200 g each)
- 2 egg yolks
- 175 g butter, chilled and cut into cubes
- 2 teaspoons finely chopped fresh tarragon
- sprigs fresh tarragon, to garnish

1 Preheat the oven to moderate 180°C (350°F/Gas 4). Cut the tomatoes into quarters and toss with the sugar, 1 tablespoon of the olive oil and 1/2 teaspoon of the salt. Spread out in a single layer in a roasting tin, then roast for 1 1/2 hours, or until slightly shrivelled and darkened. Remove from the oven and cover with foil for 15 minutes, or until cool enough to handle. Increase the oven to moderately hot 200°C (400°F/Gas 6). Peel the tomatoes, then purée and push through a sieve—you will have about 1/3 cup (80 ml) liquid.

2 Place the vinegar, peppercorns, wine and shallots in a small saucepan over medium heat and cook for 5 minutes, or until reduced to 1 tablespoon. Strain into a small heatproof bowl and set aside.

3 Peel the vegetables and cut into neat 2 cm cubes. Toss the cubes with the remaining sea salt flakes and half the remaining olive oil, then spread out in a single layer in a roasting tin. Roast for 25–30 minutes, or until crisp. Reduce the heat to very low to keep warm until ready to serve.

4 Meanwhile, tie the steaks into neat rounds, then lightly season on both sides. Heat the remaining oil in a large heavy-based frying pan over high heat, then add the steaks, making sure they are well spaced. Cook for about 4 minutes each side, or until done to your liking. Remove the string. Transfer to a warm plate, cover with foil and rest for 10–15 minutes.

5 To make the Béarnaise, whisk the egg yolks into the vinegar mixture. Sit the bowl on top of a small saucepan of barely simmering water, making sure the bowl does not touch the water and whisk for about 1 minute, or until the mixture starts to thicken, then gradually whisk in a couple of cubes of butter at a time until you have used up the butter or you have achieved a thick glossy sauce—this should take about 6–7 minutes. Remove from the heat and stir in the tomato purée and chopped tarragon. Season to taste.

6 To serve, place one quarter of the root vegetables onto each plate and top with a steak. Stir the Béarnaise, then spoon over the top, garnish with fresh tarragon and serve immediately.

NUTRITION PER SERVE
Protein 54 g; Fat 66 g; Carbohydrate 37 g; Dietary Fibre 11 g; Cholesterol 335 mg; 4105 kJ (980 cal)

Roast the tomato quarters until slightly shrivelled and darkened.

Push the cooled tomato purée through a sieve.

Cook the vinegar mixture until it has reduced to 1 tablespoon liquid.

Roast the vegetable cubes until they are crisp.

Cook the steaks in a large frying pan until cooked to your liking.

Add the butter a few cubes at a time, and whisk until thick and glossy.

DUCK BREAST ON SPICED COUSCOUS WITH RHUBARB RELISH

Preparation time: 20 minutes + 15 minutes standing
Total cooking time: 30 minutes
Serves 4

2 teaspoons butter
1 tablespoon finely chopped French shallots
1/4 teaspoon ground ginger
small pinch ground cloves
1/3 cup (80 ml) port
1 teaspoon red wine vinegar
1 tablespoon soft brown sugar
200 g rhubarb, cut into 2 cm lengths
4 duck breasts (180 g each)
1 teaspoon olive oil
1 1/2 cups (375 ml) chicken stock
1 1/2 cups (280 g) couscous
2 tablespoons butter, for pan-frying, extra
2 cloves garlic, crushed
1 teaspoon ground cumin
1 teaspoon ground cinnamon
20 g pistachios, chopped
2 tablespoons finely chopped fresh coriander leaves

1 To make the rhubarb relish, melt the butter in a saucepan over medium heat and cook the shallots for 4 minutes, or until softened. Add the ginger and cloves and stir for a further minute, or until fragrant. Stir in the port, vinegar and sugar and cook for 4 minutes, or until just syrupy, then add the rhubarb and cook for 4–5 minutes, or until just cooked through. Remove from the heat, cover and keep warm.

2 Season the duck breasts. Heat the oil in a large frying pan over medium heat and cook the duck breasts, skin-side-down, for 7 minutes, or until the skin is golden, then turn and cook for a further 2 minutes, or until tender. Flip the breasts over again, increase the heat to high and cook for 1 minute longer to make the skin crispy. Remove from the heat, cover loosely with foil and rest for 10 minutes.

3 Boil the stock in a saucepan over high heat. Remove from the heat and stir in the couscous. Place the lid on the pan and leave for 5 minutes.

4 Melt the extra butter in a small saucepan, add the garlic and spices and stir over medium heat for 1 minute. Remove the lid from the couscous, add the butter and spice mix and mix in with a fork. Stir in the pistachios and coriander. Gently reheat the rhubarb if necessary.

5 Spoon a mound of couscous onto four serving plates, top with the duck breasts and some rhubarb relish.

NUTRITION PER SERVE
Protein 40 g; Fat 25 g; Carbohydrate 57 g; Dietary Fibre 4.5 g; Cholesterol 227 mg; 2636 kJ (630 cal)

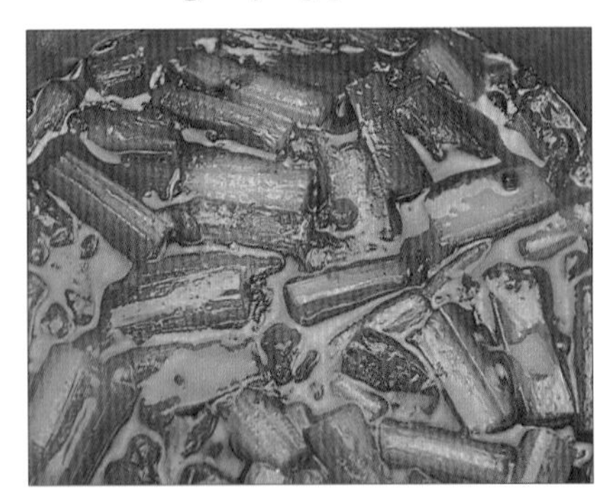

Cook the rhubarb in the syrup until it is just cooked through.

Cook the breasts, skin-side-down, until the skin is golden, then turn over.

Mix the butter and spice mixture into the couscous and fluff with a fork.

VEAL CUTLETS WITH CELERIAC PUREE AND CAPERBERRIES

Preparation time: 30 minutes + 2 hours refrigeration + 10 minutes resting
Total cooking time: 25 minutes
Serves 4

8 veal cutlets, trimmed
4 long sprigs rosemary
2 teaspoons lemon zest
1/2 cup (125 ml) white wine vinegar
1 clove garlic, crushed
1/2 cup (125 ml) lemon juice
1/4 cup (60 ml) oil
1 celeriac, peeled and chopped
750 g Pontiac potatoes, chopped
24 caperberries
lemon zest, to garnish

1 Trim the cutlets so that only the eye remains. Wrap the rosemary around four of the veal cutlets and secure with kitchen string. Place all the cutlets in a large non-metallic dish.
2 Put the lemon zest, vinegar, garlic, lemon juice and 2 tablespoons of the oil in a bowl and mix well. Pour over the cutlets, season with black pepper, cover and refrigerate for 2 hours.
3 Preheat the oven to moderately hot 200°C (400°F/Gas 6). Drain the cutlets, reserving the marinade. Heat the remaining oil in a large frying pan and cook the cutlets in batches over high heat for 2 minutes, or until brown on both sides. Transfer to a roasting tin and roast for 10–15 minutes, or until cooked to your liking. Rest for 10 minutes.
4 Meanwhile, cook the celeriac and potato in a large saucepan of boiling water for 15 minutes, or until very soft. Drain, then mash well and push through a sieve until smooth. You may need to add a little milk if it is too thick. Season with salt and pepper. Keep warm.
5 Pour the reserved marinade and caperberries into a small saucepan and bring to the boil for 2 minutes, or until slightly reduced.
6 To serve, spoon a large mound of the purée on each plate and top with a plain cutlet, then a rosemary-covered cutlet. Pour the sauce over the cutlets and add the caperberries. Garnish with lemon zest.

NUTRITION PER SERVE
Protein 88 g; Fat 22 g; Carbohydrate 32 g; Dietary Fibre 8.5 g; Cholesterol 300 mg; 2904 kJ (694 cal)

Wrap the rosemary around half of the cutlets and secure with string.

Cook the potato and celeriac until they are very soft.

LAMB BACKSTRAPS ON EGGPLANT MASH AND OLIVE SALSA

Preparation time: 45 minutes + overnight refrigeration + 10 minutes resting
Total cooking time: 3 hours
Serves 4

2 tablespoons lemon juice
2 teaspoons ground cumin
1/2 cup (125 ml) olive oil
4 lamb backstraps or loin fillets (200 g each), trimmed
1 kg lamb bones
1 onion, chopped
3 cloves garlic, peeled and bruised
1 carrot, chopped
1 celery stick, chopped
1 bay leaf
1 cup (250 ml) white wine
2 1/2 tablespoons ground cumin, extra
2 large eggplants
500 g desirée potatoes
2 teaspoons tahini
1/4 teaspoon sesame oil
3 cloves garlic, crushed, extra

Olive salsa
2/3 cup (12 g) fresh mint, finely chopped
2 tablespoons finely chopped pitted black olives
2 tablespoons finely diced red capsicum
1 tablespoon sesame seeds, toasted
1 tablespoon finely chopped red onion

1 To make the marinade, put the lemon juice, cumin and 2 tablespoons of the olive oil in a flat non-metallic, shallow dish and mix together. Add the lamb backstraps and stir to coat them well. Cover and refrigerate overnight.

2 Preheat the oven to hot 220°C (425°F/Gas 7). Pour 1 tablespoon of the remaining oil into a very large saucepan over medium heat, add the lamb bones and cook for a few minutes, or until well browned. Add the onion, garlic, carrot, celery, bay leaf, wine and extra cumin to the pan and stir well. Cover with cold water and bring to the boil, then reduce the heat and simmer for 2 hours, skimming off any scum that forms on the surface. Remove the bones, then strain the stock through a fine sieve into a smaller saucepan and leave off the heat for 10 minutes, then remove any fat that has settled on top. Simmer for an hour, or until the sauce thickens slightly—you should have about 1/3 cup (80 ml) sauce. Remove from the heat, season to taste, cover and keep warm.

3 Meanwhile, prick the eggplants all over with a fork, then place in a roasting tin and cook in the preheated oven for 45 minutes, or until they are quite wrinkled. Remove from the oven and place in a colander over a bowl to catch the drips from any bitter juices. Reduce the oven temperature to moderately hot 190°C (375°F/Gas 5). When the eggplants are cool enough to handle comfortably, cut them in half and carefully scoop out the flesh. Process the flesh in a food processor until smooth.

4 Roughly chop the potatoes, then place them in a saucepan. Cover the potato with cold water, then bring to the boil and cook for 12 minutes, or until soft. Drain well, then add the tahini, sesame oil, extra garlic and 2 tablespoons of the remaining olive oil. Mash well, then season to taste with salt and cracked black pepper. Stir in the eggplant purée.

5 To make the olive salsa, combine all the ingredients in a bowl and season to taste.

6 Heat the remaining oil in a large heavy-based frying pan over high heat, then add the lamb backstraps in batches, spacing them well apart. Cook each side for 2 minutes. Remove from the pan and place in a roasting tin in the oven for 5 minutes for a medium–rare result, or until cooked to your liking. Remove from the oven, cover with foil and rest for 10 minutes. Reheat the mash if needed.

7 To serve, place a large spoonful of the eggplant mash on each plate. Drain any juices from the rested lamb into the sauce and bring to a simmer. Slice the very ends off each backstrap, then cut on a slight angle into thin slices. Overlap the slices on the mash and top with one quarter of the olive salsa. Drizzle the sauce around the edge of the plate.

Cook the lamb bones until they are well browned.

Simmer the sauce until it has thickened slightly.

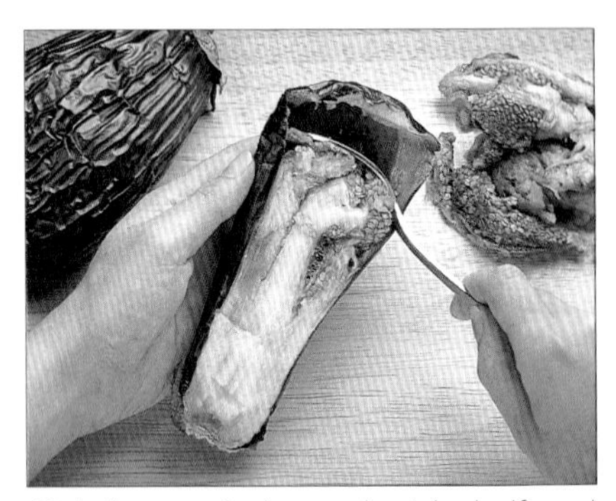

Cut the cooled eggplant in half and scoop out the flesh.

Stir the eggplant purée through the potato mash.

NUTRITION PER SERVE
Protein 50 g; Fat 40 g; Carbohydrate 25 g; Dietary Fibre 9 g; Cholesterol 132 mg; 2927 kJ (699 cal)

BEEF FILLET WITH ONION MARMALADE AND CREAMY POTATO GRATIN

Preparation time: 30 minutes + 2 hours refrigeration
Total cooking time: 1 hour 10 minutes
Serves 4

1 cup (250 ml) port
1/4 cup (60 ml) balsamic vinegar
2 cloves garlic, crushed
4 beef eye fillet steaks
1 tablespoon olive oil

Onion marmalade
1/4 cup (60 ml) olive oil
500 g onions, thinly sliced
1/4 cup (45 g) soft brown sugar
75 ml red wine vinegar

Potato gratin
4 large potatoes, thinly sliced
1 onion, thinly sliced
1 cup (250 ml) cream
50 g Gruyère cheese, grated

1 Put the port, vinegar and garlic in a non-metallic dish and mix together well. Add the beef and stir to coat. Cover and refrigerate for 2 hours. Drain, reserving the marinade.
2 To make the marmalade, heat the oil in a large non-stick frying pan, add the onion and sugar and cook over medium heat for 30–40 minutes, or until caramelised. Stir in the red wine vinegar, bring to the boil and cook for 10 minutes, or until thick and sticky. Remove from the heat and keep warm.
3 Meanwhile, preheat the oven to moderate 180°C (350°F/Gas 4). Lightly grease four 1/2 cup (125 ml) soufflé dishes, then fill with alternating layers of potato and onion. Mix the cream and cheese together in a bowl and season, then pour into the dishes. Place on a baking tray and bake for 45 minutes, or until the potato is cooked. Remove from the heat and keep warm.
4 Heat the oil in a large frying pan, add the steaks and cook over high heat for 3–5 minutes each side, or until cooked to your liking. Remove from the pan and keep warm, then add the reserved marinade to the pan and boil for 5–6 minutes, or until reduced by half.
5 Spoon some of the sauce onto four serving plates, place a steak on the sauce, top with a generous mound of onion marmalade and a gratin. Serve with steamed greens.

NUTRITION PER SERVE
Protein 53 g; Fat 59 g; Carbohydrate 43 g; Dietary Fibre 4.5 g; Cholesterol 232 mg; 4048 kJ (967 cal)

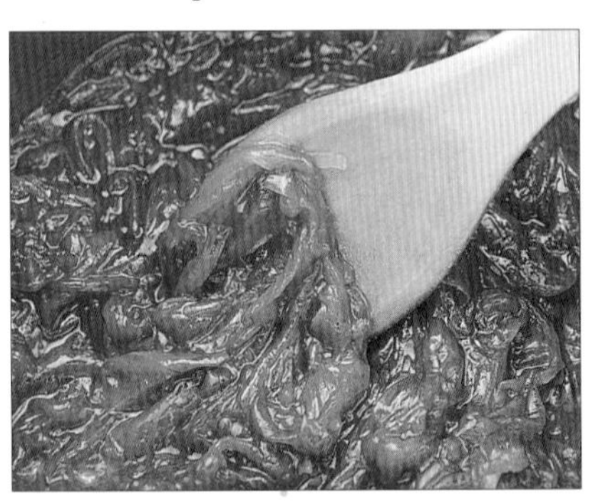

Cook the onion marmalade until thick and sticky.

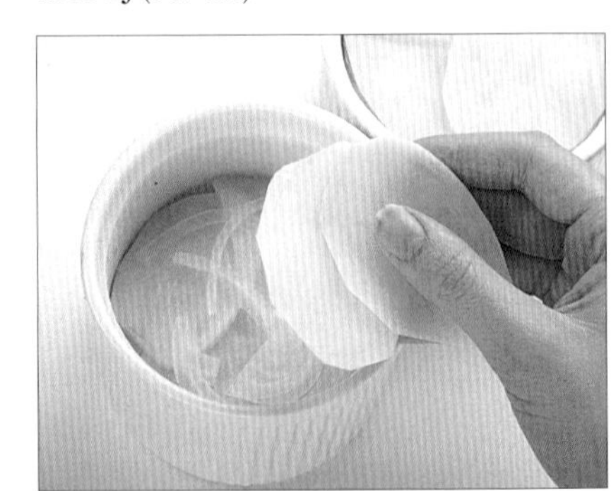

Lay alternate layers of potato and onion in the soufflé dishes.

CORN-FED CHICKEN BREASTS WITH LENTILS AND STAR ANISE JUS

Preparation time: 20 minutes + 10 minutes standing
Total cooking time: 2 hours 40 minutes
Serve[illegible] 4

2–3 [illegible] arcasses
2 [illegible]
2 [illegible]
2 [illegible]
1 [illegible] ive oil
[illegible] bruised
[illegible] hyme
[illegible] puy lentils
[illegible], crushed, extra
[illegible] chopped fresh thyme
[illegible] icken breast fillets
[illegible] ithout wing bone)

1 [illegible]e the jus, chop the [illegible]nto large pieces. Roughly [illegible] onion, carrot and celery [illegible]t 1 tablespoon of the oil in a ver[illegible]ge saucepan over medium heat. Add the chopped onion, carrot and celery and cook for about 4 minutes, or until they start to brown, then remove from the pan. Add another tablespoon of the oil and the chicken bones to the pan and cook, stirring, for about 5 minutes, or until well browned. Return the vegetables to the pan and add the star anise, bruised garlic, thyme sprigs and 2.5 litres cold water. Bring to the boil, reduce the heat and simmer for 1 1/2 hours, removing any scum that forms on the top.

2 Strain into a clean saucepan and simmer over medium heat for 1 hour, or until slightly thick—you should have 2/3 cup (170 ml) jus. Remove from the heat, cover and keep warm.

3 Meanwhile, prepare the rest of the meal. Rinse the lentils under running water, then put in a large saucepan and cover with cold water. Bring slowly to the boil, then simmer over medium heat for 20–25 minutes, or until tender but not mushy. Drain. Finely chop the remaining onion and dice the carrot and celery stick.

4 Heat another tablespoon of the oil in a large frying pan over medium heat, add the bay leaf and onion and cook for 3 minutes, then add the carrot and celery and cook for 5 minutes, stirring, until softened and lightly browned. Stir in the extra garlic and the chopped thyme and cook for 1 minute. Gently fold in the lentils, stirring carefully for 2 minutes to heat through. Season, then remove from the heat and cover with foil to keep warm.

5 Heat the remaining oil in a large frying pan over high heat. Season the chicken breasts with salt and black pepper, then cook, skin-side-down, for 5 minutes. Turn over, reduce the heat to medium and cook for a further 5 minutes, or until tender. Remove from the heat and rest for 10 minutes.

6 Place a mound of lentils on each plate, top with the chicken and spoon the jus around the plate.

NUTRITION PER SERVE
Protein 62 g; Fat 25 g; Carbohydrate 20 g; Dietary Fibre 9 g; Cholesterol 110 mg; 2337 kJ (558 cal)

Simmer the strained stock until thickened slightly.

Add the lentils to the vegetable mixture and stir gently until heated through.

CRISPY-SKINNED SALMON WITH TOMATO FENNEL DRESSING

Preparation time: 20 minutes
Total cooking time: 25 minutes
Serves 4

- 2 ripe tomatoes
- 1 kg King Edward potatoes, chopped
- 100 g butter
- 100 ml milk or cream, warmed
- 1 tablespoon chopped fresh chervil
- 1 tablespoon chopped fresh tarragon
- 1/3 cup (80 ml) olive oil
- 2 spring onions, finely chopped
- 1 bulb baby fennel, finely chopped
- 1 tablespoon baby capers
- 2 tablespoons red wine vinegar
- 4 salmon fillets or ocean trout fillets, skin on (150 g each)

1 Score a cross in the base of the tomatoes, place in a heatproof bowl and cover with boiling water. Leave for 10 seconds, then transfer to cold water and peel the skin away from the cross. Cut in half and scoop out the seeds with a teaspoon. Chop.

2 Cook the potatoes in a large saucepan of boiling water for 15 minutes, or until soft. Drain well and return to the heat until all the moisture has been absorbed. Remove from the heat and mash smooth. Add the butter and gradually beat in the milk with a wooden spoon. Stir in the herbs, season, cover and keep warm.

3 Meanwhile, heat 1 tablespoon of the oil in a large frying pan, add the spring onion and fennel and cook over medium heat for 10 minutes, or until very soft, then add the tomato, capers and vinegar and bring to the boil for 1 minute. Do not overcook or the tomatoes will go mushy. Remove from the heat and keep warm.

4 Pat the fillets dry with paper towels and rub the skin with a little salt. Heat the remaining oil in a large frying pan, add the fillets, skin-side-down, and cook over medium heat for 2–3 minutes, or until very crisp, then turn and cook for 2 minutes for a medium–rare result.

5 Serve, skin-side-up, on a bed of mash with the dressing. (The dressing may soften the skin if served on top.)

NUTRITION PER SERVE
Protein 45 g; Fat 45 g; Carbohydrate 36 g; Dietary Fibre 5 g; Cholesterol 184 mg; 3067 kJ (733 cal)

Peel the skin away from the cross at the base of the tomato.

Cut the tomatoes in half and scoop the seeds out with a teaspoon.

Cook the fillets until the skin is crisp, then turn and cook the other side.

LAMB CUTLETS WITH BEETROOT, BEAN AND POTATO SALAD

Preparation time: 15 minutes + overnight refrigeration
Total cooking time: 35 minutes
Serves 4

2 cloves garlic, crushed
2 tablespoons finely chopped fresh thyme
1 1/2 tablespoons lemon juice
1 tablespoon walnut oil
2 tablespoons extra virgin olive oil
12 lamb cutlets, trimmed
6 baby beetroots, trimmed
500 g kipfler potatoes, unpeeled
250 g baby green beans
2 tablespoons olive oil

Dressing
1 clove garlic, crushed
3 1/2 tablespoons lemon juice
1/3 cup (80 ml) extra virgin olive oil
1 tablespoon walnut oil
1/4 cup (30 g) chopped walnuts

1 Combine the garlic, thyme, lemon juice, walnut oil and extra virgin olive oil in a shallow, non-metallic dish, add the cutlets and toss well. Cover with plastic wrap and refrigerate overnight.
2 Cook the beetroots in boiling water for 20 minutes, or until tender. Drain. Meanwhile, cook the potatoes in lightly salted boiling water for 12 minutes, or until tender. Drain.
3 When cool enough to handle, peel the beetroots and potatoes. Cut each beetroot into six wedges and thickly slice the potatoes.
4 Cook the beans in lightly salted boiling water for 4 minutes. Drain, refresh under cold water, then drain again. Pat dry with paper towels.
5 Heat the olive oil in a large frying pan over high heat and cook the cutlets in batches for 4–5 minutes, or until cooked to your liking, turning once.
6 Whisk the garlic, lemon juice, extra virgin olive oil and walnut oil in a large bowl. Add the potatoes, beans and walnuts and toss gently. Season and arrange over the beetroot. Top with the cutlets and serve.

NUTRITION PER SERVE
Protein 30 g; Fat 55 g; Carbohydrate 25 g; Dietary Fibre 6.5 g; Cholesterol 70 mg; 2990 kJ (714 cal)

Peel the beetroots and cut each one into six wedges.

Cook the cutlets in batches until done to your liking.

Clockwise from top left: Chats with aïoli, Stir-fried vegetables, Spinach with garlic butter, Beans with pecorino, Creamy mashed potato, Roasted spiced sweet potato wedges.

Vegetables on the side

Add a plate of steaming mashed potato, a bowl of delicious stir-fried vegetables or some roasted wedges to the table and transform your meal into a true feast. Each side dish serves 4–6 people.

CHATS WITH AIOLI

Combine 3/4 cup (185 g) whole-egg mayonnaise with 3–4 cloves crushed garlic, 2 tablespoons lemon juice and 1 tablespoon finely chopped fresh parsley, then season. Boil 1 kg whole chat or other small washed potatoes for 10 minutes, or until almost cooked. Drain and leave until cool enough to handle. Fill a large heavy-based saucepan half full of oil and heat until a cube of bread browns in 15 seconds. Break the chats into halves with your hands, then deep-fry in batches until crisp and golden. Drain on paper towels and sprinkle with sea salt flakes. Serve with the aïoli.

ROASTED SPICED SWEET POTATO WEDGES

Cut 1 kg orange sweet potato into wedges. Combine 2 teaspoons ground cumin, 1/2 teaspoon cayenne pepper, 1 teaspoon paprika, 3 teaspoons salt and 1/4 cup (60 ml) oil in a large bowl, add the wedges and toss. Put in a single layer in a roasting tin and cook in a moderately hot (200°C/400°F/Gas 6) oven for 35 minutes, or until crisp and golden but soft in the centre.

CREAMY MASHED POTATO

Cut 1 kg desirée potatoes into quarters and boil in a large saucepan of water for 12 minutes, or until soft. Drain, then return to the heat, shaking to dry any excess water. Add 2–3 tablespoons butter and 3/4 cup (185 g) sour cream and mash with a potato masher until smooth and lump-free. Season to taste.

STIR-FRIED VEGETABLES

Heat a wok over high heat, add 1 tablespoon peanut oil and swirl to coat. Add 1 teaspoon each of finely chopped garlic and ginger. Cut 155 g thin asparagus into 3 cm lengths. Thinly slice 1 carrot on the diagonal and chop 1 small red capsicum. Stir-fry the carrot and capsicum for 1 minute, then add 100 g halved snow peas, the asparagus lengths and 4 sliced spring onions. Stir-fry the vegetables for 1 minute. Combine 2 teaspoons each of oyster sauce, soy sauce and mirin, pour into the wok and cook for 1 minute. Add 50 g snow pea sprouts and stir until just wilted, then remove from the heat and serve.

SPINACH WITH GARLIC BUTTER

Rinse and drain 750 g baby English spinach leaves. Dry on a tea towel. Heat 2–3 tablespoons of butter with 2 cloves crushed garlic and 1/4 teaspoon nutmeg until the butter begins to froth. Add the spinach leaves and toss until just wilted. Season and serve immediately.

BEANS WITH PECORINO

Trim 200 g each of green and yellow butter beans, then plunge into boiling water with 1 teaspoon salt for 4 minutes, or until tender but still crisp. Drain, then quickly refresh under cold running water. Toss with 1 tablespoon extra virgin olive oil and season to taste with salt. Place in a serving dish and top with 40 g shaved pecorino cheese.

SNAPPER FILLETS WITH TOMATO JAM ON WHITE BEAN SKORDALIA

Preparation time: 20 minutes
Total cooking time: 45 minutes
Serves 4

Tomato jam
1 tablespoon olive oil
1 small onion, finely chopped
2 cloves garlic, crushed
1 teaspoon yellow mustard seeds
400 g Roma tomatoes, chopped
1 1/2 tablespoons caster sugar
1/3 cup (80 ml) semi-sweet sherry
2 teaspoons red wine vinegar
2 teaspoons finely chopped fresh oregano

Skordalia
2 x 400 g cans cannellini beans, rinsed and drained
1/2 cup (95 g) ground almonds
1 tablespoon lemon juice
3 cloves garlic, chopped
1/2 cup (125 ml) olive oil
1 teaspoon finely chopped fresh oregano

Snapper fillets
1 tablespoon olive oil, for pan-frying
4 pieces snapper fillet (150–200 g each), skin on
black olives, to garnish
fresh oregano, to garnish
extra virgin olive oil, to serve

1 To make the jam, heat the oil in a saucepan over medium heat. Cook the onion for 5 minutes, or until lightly browned, then add the garlic and mustard and stir for 1 minute, or until fragrant. Add the tomato, sugar, sherry, vinegar, oregano, 2 tablespoons water and some salt. Reduce to a simmer and cook, stirring often, for 30 minutes, or until pulpy. Remove from the heat, cover and keep warm.

2 Meanwhile, to make the skordalia, place the beans, almonds, lemon juice and garlic in a food processor and process until smooth. While the motor is running, gradually add the oil and process until thick and creamy. Transfer to a saucepan over low heat and stir until heated through. Season, cover and keep warm.

3 Heat the oil in a large frying pan over medium heat. Sprinkle the skin of the snapper with some salt, then add to the pan, skin-side-down and cook for 2–3 minutes each side.

4 To serve, stir the oregano through the skordalia, place a large spoonful on each plate, top with the snapper and a dollop of the jam. Garnish with olives and oregano and drizzle a little extra virgin olive oil around the plate.

NUTRITION PER SERVE
Protein 60 g; Fat 56 g; Carbohydrate 34 g; Dietary Fibre 18 g; Cholesterol 122 mg; 3682 kJ (880 cal)

Simmer the tomato jam until it is thick and pulpy.

Process the skordalia ingredients until thick and creamy.

Cook the snapper, skin-side-down, then turn.

LEMON ROASTED SPATCHCOCK WITH ZUCCHINI PANCAKES

Preparation time: 30 minutes + overnight refrigeration + 40 minutes standing
Total cooking time: 1 hour
Serves 4

1 cup (60 g) finely chopped fresh basil
2 cloves garlic, crushed
2 teaspoons grated lemon rind
1/4 cup (60 ml) olive oil
4 spatchcocks (see Note)

Zucchini pancakes
700 g zucchini
4 eggs
40 g Parmesan, grated
1/3 cup (40 g) plain flour
1 clove garlic, crushed
1/2 cup (15 g) chopped fresh flat-leaf parsley
2 tablespoons olive oil

Tomato and black olive relish
2 large ripe tomatoes, seeded and diced
1/2 cup (60 g) sliced black olives
1 1/2 tablespoons extra virgin olive oil
2 cloves garlic, crushed
2 tablespoons finely chopped fresh flat-leaf parsley

1 Put the basil, garlic, lemon rind, 1 teaspoon salt and 1/2 teaspoon cracked black pepper in a large non-metallic dish and mix. Whisk in the oil. Rub under and over the spatchcock skin. Cover and refrigerate overnight.
2 Slice both ends off the zucchini but don't peel. Grate on the coarse side of a grater. Toss with salt and sit in a colander for 30 minutes.
3 Preheat the oven to moderately hot 190°C (375°F/Gas 5). Grease a large chargrill pan and cook the spatchcocks one or two at a time over medium heat for 5 minutes each side, or until golden. Transfer to a large roasting tin and roast for 10–12 minutes, or until the juices run clear when the inside of a thigh is pierced. Remove from the oven, cover with foil and rest for 10 minutes.
4 Rinse the salt off the zucchini and squeeze to remove any excess liquid. Mix the zucchini with the eggs, Parmesan, flour, garlic, parsley and 1 teaspoon salt. Season to taste with pepper. Heat half the oil in a non-stick frying pan over medium heat. Form two pancakes (each using about 3 tablespoons batter) and cook for 2 1/2 minutes each side, or until golden. Drain on paper towels and repeat with the remaining oil and batter to make six more pancakes.
5 To make the relish, combine all the ingredients in a bowl. Season to taste.

Chargrill the spatchcocks in batches until golden.

6 Carve the spatchcock into four and serve with two zucchini cakes and a dollop of the relish.

NUTRITION PER SERVE
Protein 30 g; Fat 48 g; Carbohydrate 12 g; Dietary Fibre 5 g; Cholesterol 370 mg; 2215 kJ (530 cal)

COOK'S FILE

NOTE: A spatchcock is a very young chicken weighing about 0.5 kg. The term also means the method of splitting it down the back and flattening it.

Cook the zucchini pancakes until nicely browned.

LAMB CUTLETS WITH PARMESAN POLENTA AND RATATOUILLE

Preparation time: 25 minutes + 10 minutes cooling
Total cooking time: 2 hours 35 minutes
Serves 4

- 1 kg lamb bones
- 1 onion, chopped
- 1 large carrot, chopped
- 1 celery stick, chopped
- 1 bay leaf
- 1 teaspoon black peppercorns
- 4 cloves garlic, peeled and bruised
- 6 Roma tomatoes, chopped
- 1 cup (250 ml) red wine
- 2 cups (500 ml) sherry
- 4 sprigs fresh thyme
- 1 red onion
- 1 eggplant
- 1 small red capsicum
- 1 small green capsicum
- 1 small yellow capsicum
- 1 zucchini
- 1 tablespoon finely chopped fresh thyme
- 2 tablespoons olive oil
- 1 litre chicken stock
- 1 cup (170 g) instant polenta
- 2 tablespoons butter
- 1/2 cup (50 g) finely grated Parmesan
- 2 tablespoons olive oil, for pan-frying, extra
- 12 lamb cutlets
- 2 tablespoons finely chopped fresh parsley

1 Cook the lamb bones in a large saucepan over medium heat, stirring occasionally for 5 minutes, or until browned. Add the onion, carrot, celery, bay leaf, peppercorns, garlic, tomato, wine, sherry, thyme and 1 litre cold water. Bring to the boil, then reduce the heat and simmer for 2 hours, skimming off any scum. Remove the bones, then strain into a saucepan and simmer for 30 minutes, or until thickened—you should have about 3/4 cup (185 ml) sauce. Remove from the heat, cover and keep warm.

2 Meanwhile, preheat the oven to moderately hot 200°C (400°F/Gas 6). To make the ratatouille, cut the red onion, eggplant, capsicums and zucchini into 1.5 cm cubes and combine in a large roasting tin. Add the thyme and drizzle with the oil. Season, then spread out in a single layer. Roast, stirring occasionally, for 30–35 minutes, or until just cooked and starting to brown. Remove from the oven and cover with foil. Reduce the heat to moderate 180°C (350°F/Gas 4).

3 While the ratatouille is cooking, bring the chicken stock to the boil, then slowly pour in the polenta, stirring constantly. Cook, stirring, for 8–10 minutes, or until the polenta is smooth and thick. Stir in the butter and Parmesan. Season and keep warm.

4 Heat 1 tablespoon of the extra olive oil in a large frying pan over high heat and sear half the cutlets for 1 minute each side, then place in a single layer in a roasting tin. Repeat with the remaining cutlets. Bake for 4–5 minutes for a medium–rare result. Remove from the oven, cover and rest for 10 minutes. If necessary, reheat the ratatouille in the oven for 5 minutes. Stir in the parsley just before serving.

5 To serve, dollop polenta onto each plate, top with three cutlets and some ratatouille. Drizzle with the sauce.

NUTRITION PER SERVE
Protein 35 g; Fat 39 g; Carbohydrate 42 g; Dietary Fibre 8 g; Cholesterol 105 mg; 3466 kJ (828 cal)

Cook the lamb bones until they are well browned.

Simmer the liquid, skimming off any scum that forms on top.

Simmer the strained liquid in a clean saucepan until just thickened.

Toss the vegetables, thyme and oil together, then cook until just browned.

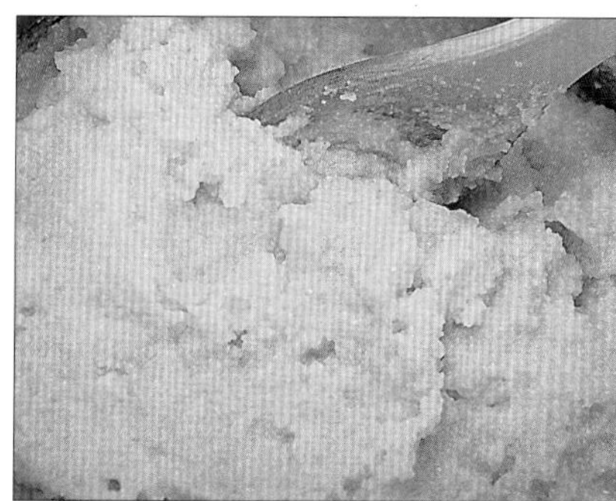
Cook the polenta, stirring constantly, until it is smooth and thick.

Sear the lamb cutlets in batches for 1 minute each side.

THAI-SPICED GRILLED PORK TENDERLOIN AND GREEN MANGO SALAD

Preparation time: 45 minutes + 2 hours refrigeration
Total cooking time: 10 minutes
Serves 4 as a main (6 as an entrée)

- 2 stems lemon grass (white part only), thinly sliced
- 1 clove garlic
- 2 red Asian shallots
- 1 tablespoon coarsely chopped fresh ginger
- 1 red bird's-eye chilli, seeded
- 1 tablespoon fish sauce
- 1/2 cup (15 g) fresh coriander
- 1 teaspoon grated lime rind
- 1 tablespoon lime juice
- 2 tablespoons oil
- 2 pork tenderloins, trimmed
- steamed jasmine rice (optional)

Dressing

- 1 large red chilli, seeded and finely chopped
- 2 cloves garlic, finely chopped
- 3 fresh coriander roots, finely chopped
- 1 1/4 tablespoons grated palm sugar
- 2 tablespoons fish sauce
- 1/4 cup (60 ml) lime juice

Salad

- 2 green mangoes or 1 small green papaya, peeled, pitted and cut into julienne strips
- 1 carrot, grated
- 1/2 cup (45 g) bean sprouts
- 1/2 red onion, thinly sliced
- 3 tablespoons roughly chopped fresh mint
- 3 tablespoons roughly chopped fresh coriander leaves
- 3 tablespoons roughly chopped fresh Vietnamese mint

1 Place the lemon grass, garlic, shallots, ginger, chilli, fish sauce, coriander, lime rind, lime juice and oil in a blender or food processor and process until a coarse paste forms. Transfer to a non-metallic dish. Coat the pork in the marinade, cover and refrigerate for at least 2 hours, but no longer than 4 hours.

2 To make the salad dressing, mix all the ingredients together in a bowl.

3 Combine all the salad ingredients in a large bowl.

4 Preheat a grill or chargrill pan and cook the pork over medium heat for 4–5 minutes each side, or until cooked through. Remove from the heat, rest for 5 minutes, then slice.

5 Toss the dressing and salad together. Season to taste with salt and cracked black pepper. Arrange the sliced pork in a circle in the centre of each plate and top with salad. To make this a main course, serve with steamed jasmine rice, if desired.

NUTRITION PER SERVE (4)
Protein 60 g; Fat 14 g; Carbohydrate 20 g; Dietary Fibre 3 g; Cholesterol 122 mg; 1860 kJ (444 cal)

Process the marinade ingredients to a coarse paste.

Cook the pork on a chargrill pan until cooked through.

POACHED COCONUT CHICKEN

Preparation time: 5 minutes + 10 minutes resting
Total cooking time: 20 minutes
Serves 4

400 ml coconut milk
2 tablespoons fish sauce
1 1/2 tablespoons grated palm sugar
1 tablespoon green peppercorns, drained and gently crushed
1 stem lemon grass (white part only), split lengthways and bruised
4 chicken breast fillets, skin removed
lime wedges, to serve

1 Place the coconut milk, fish sauce, sugar, peppercorns and lemon grass in a large saucepan and cook, stirring, over medium heat for 2 minutes, or until the sugar dissolves. Reduce the heat and keep at a low simmer.
2 Add the chicken fillets and cook for 10–15 minutes, turning halfway. To check if the fillet is cooked, press the thickest section with your fingertips. The flesh should be springy to touch—if not, cook for 2 minutes. Remove from the heat and rest for 10 minutes.
3 Cut the fillets into thick slices and divide among four plates. (You can remove the lemon grass, if you prefer.) Spoon the liquid over the chicken. Serve the chicken with lime wedges and jasmine rice, if desired.

NUTRITION PER SERVE
Protein 52 g; Fat 25 g; Carbohydrate 11 g; Dietary Fibre 2 g; Cholesterol 110 mg; 2005 kJ (480 cal)

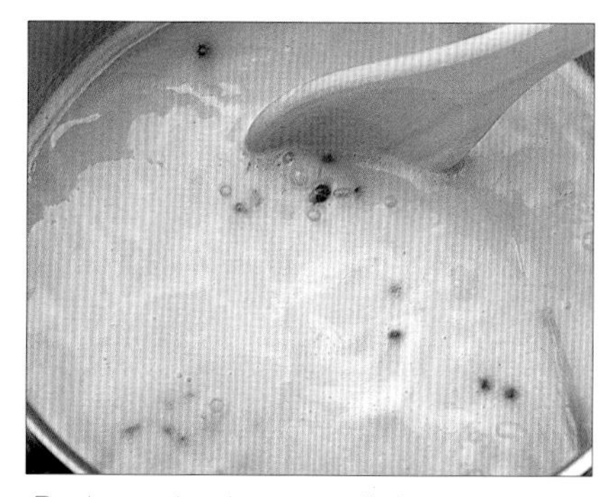

Reduce the heat until the poaching liquid is at a simmer.

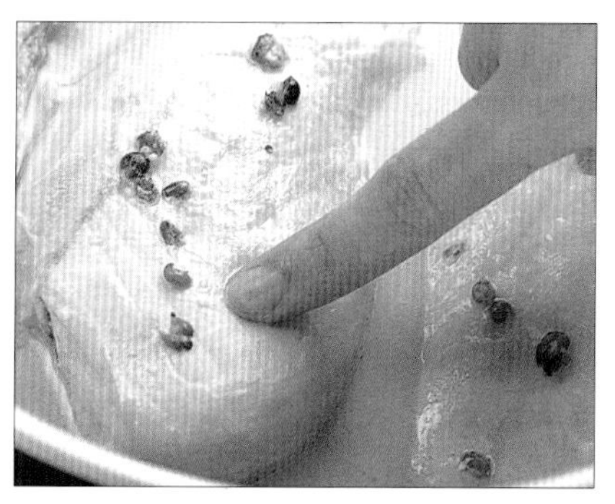

Press the thickest section of the chicken with your fingertips.

Cut the chicken into thick slices on a slight angle.

BEEF RIB ROAST WITH GARLIC BREAD & BUTTER PUDDINGS

Preparation time: 35 minutes + 35 minutes standing
Total cooking time: 2 hours
Serves 4

Beetroot relish
3 baby beetroots (200 g in total)
1 teaspoon sea salt flakes
1 tablespoon olive oil
2–3 teaspoons horseradish cream
10 g gherkin, finely chopped
1 clove garlic, crushed
2 teaspoons red wine vinegar
2 teaspoons whole-egg mayonnaise
2 tablespoons finely chopped fresh flat-leaf parsley

Rib roast
1.5–1.75 kg beef standing rib roast (4 racks), very well trimmed
2 tablespoons olive oil
1 tablespoon flour
1 cup (250 ml) red wine
1 cup (250 ml) beef stock
1 tablespoon green peppercorns

Garlic bread and butter puddings
1/4 cup (60 ml) milk
1/2 cup (125 ml) cream
10 cloves garlic, chopped
1 egg
1 tablespoon finely chopped fresh flat-leaf parsley, extra
softened butter, to spread
6 slices white bread

1 Preheat the oven to moderately hot 200°C (400°F/Gas 6). To make the beetroot relish, trim the beetroots and cut them into halves. Toss with the salt and oil in a roasting tin and cook for 40–45 minutes, or until tender when tested with the point of a knife. Remove from the oven and cover with foil until cool enough to handle. Reduce the oven to moderately hot 190°C (375°F/Gas 5).

2 Peel and coarsely grate the beetroot, then place in a bowl with the horseradish, gherkin, garlic, vinegar, mayonnaise and parsley, then mix well and season. Cover and set aside.

3 Season the beef well. Pour the oil into a large heavy-based frying pan over high heat, then sear the beef for 2 minutes each side, or until well browned. Transfer the beef to a roasting tin, setting the frying pan aside to use for the sauce. Roast the beef for 1 hour until medium–rare, or until cooked to your liking. (The cooking time will vary depending on the size of the roast.) Remove from the oven and rest for 20 minutes. Leave the oven on.

4 Meanwhile, to make the bread and butter puddings, combine the milk, cream and garlic in a saucepan and bring to the boil, then reduce the heat and simmer for 10 minutes. Remove from the heat and leave to infuse for 15 minutes. Strain the mixture into a jug. Whisk in the egg and the extra parsley and season.

5 Lightly butter the bread on both sides, then remove the crusts and cut the bread into 1.5 cm squares. Press the bread into four 1/2 cup (125 ml) muffin holes and gradually pour the custard over them, allowing the bread to absorb the custard before each addition. Leave for 15 minutes.

6 While the meat is resting, place the bread and butter puddings in the oven and cook for 12 minutes, or until puffed and golden. Remove from the muffin holes with a flat-bladed knife.

7 Meanwhile, reheat the frying pan in which the beef was cooked. Sprinkle the pan with flour and stir over medium heat for 1 minute, then add the wine and stock. Scrape up any sediment and cook for 6–8 minutes, or until thickened slightly. Stir in the green peppercorns. Season well and remove from the heat, then cover and set aside.

8 Add any juices from the rested meat to the sauce and reheat gently. Cut down between the racks of beef, dividing into four even pieces. Arrange on a plate with the pudding and a little beetroot relish, then drizzle the peppercorn sauce over the meat and around the plate.

NUTRITION PER SERVE
Protein 103 g; Fat 55 g; Carbohydrate 30 g; Dietary Fibre 3.5 g; Cholesterol 318 mg; 4421 kJ (1056 cal)

COOK'S FILE

VARIATION: You can make carrot relish instead of the beetroot. Use the same method but use 200 g carrot and substitute dill for the parsley.

When cool enough to handle, peel the beetroots, then coarsely grate them.

Sear the beef for 2 minutes each side, or until well browned.

Press the bread cubes into the four muffin holes.

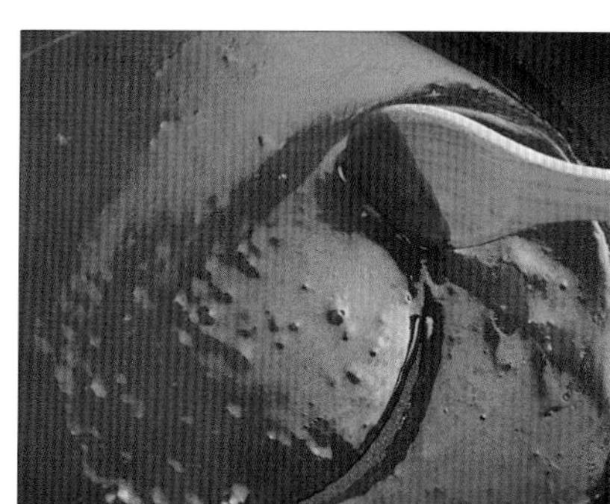

Cook the sauce, stirring, until it thickens slightly.

TERIYAKI PORK WITH SOYA BEANS

Preparation time: 20 minutes + 2 hours refrigeration + 10 minutes resting
Total cooking time: 30 minutes
Serves 4

1 1/2 tablespoons soy sauce
3 teaspoons grated fresh ginger
1 clove garlic, crushed
1/4 cup (60 ml) peanut oil
1/4 cup (60 ml) dry sherry
700 g pork fillet
2 tablespoons honey
300 g frozen soya beans
4 baby bok choy, sliced in half lengthways
3 teaspoons sesame oil
2 teaspoons finely chopped fresh ginger, extra
1 clove garlic, crushed, extra
sesame seeds, toasted, to garnish (optional)

1 Place the soy sauce, ginger, garlic and 2 tablespoons each of the peanut oil and sherry in a large shallow non-metallic dish and mix well. Add the pork and toss gently to coat well. Cover and refrigerate for 2 hours, turning the meat occasionally. Preheat the oven to moderate 180°C (350°F/Gas 4).
2 Remove the pork and drain well, reserving the marinade. Pat the pork dry with paper towels. Heat the remaining peanut oil in a large frying pan and cook the pork over medium heat for 5–6 minutes, or until browned all over. Transfer to a baking tray and roast for 10–15 minutes. Cover with foil and rest for 10 minutes.
3 Put the reserved marinade, honey, the remaining sherry and 1/3 cup (80 ml) water in a small saucepan and bring to the boil. Reduce the heat and simmer for 3–4 minutes, or until reduced to a glaze. Keep the glaze hot.
4 Cook the soya beans in a large covered saucepan of lightly salted boiling water for 1 minute, then add the bok choy and cook for a further 2 minutes. Drain. Heat the sesame oil in the same saucepan, add the extra ginger and garlic and heat for 30 seconds. Return the soya beans and bok choy to the pan and toss gently.
5 Slice the pork. Put the vegetables on a large serving dish and top with the pork slices. Spoon the glaze over the pork, sprinkle with sesame seeds and serve immediately.

NUTRITION PER SERVE
Protein 48 g; Fat 25 g; Carbohydrate 6.5 g; Dietary Fibre 5 g; Cholesterol 86 mg; 1899 kJ (455 cal)

Cook the pork fillets until browned all over.

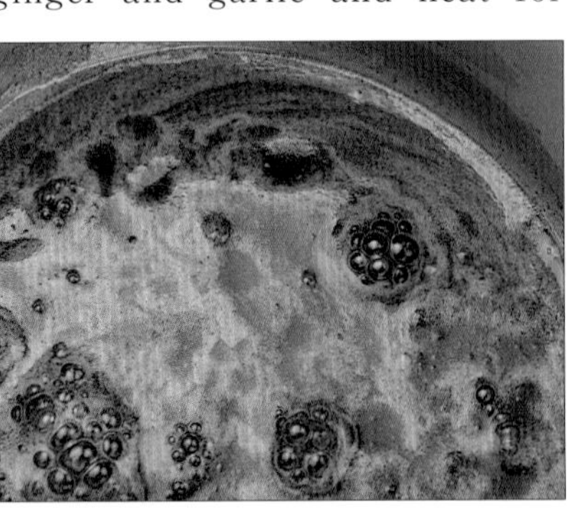

Simmer the marinade, honey and sherry mixture until reduced to a glaze.

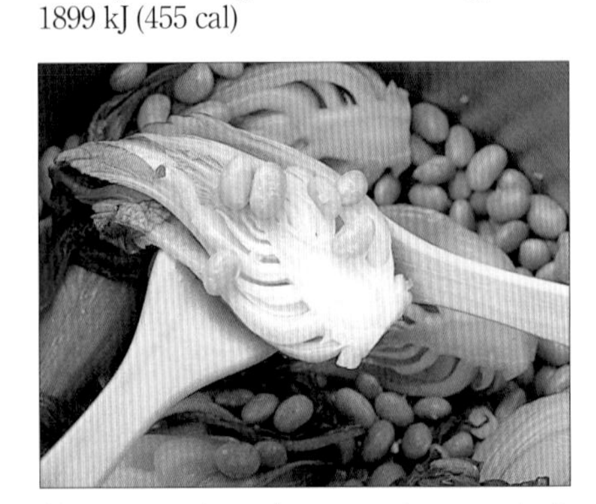

Toss together the soya beans, bok choy, ginger and garlic.

FIVE-SPICE BEEF WITH ASIAN MUSHROOMS

Preparation time: 20 minutes + 10 minutes resting
Total cooking time: 30 minutes
Serves 4

1/4 cup (60 ml) soy sauce
1/4 cup (60 ml) mirin
1/4 cup (60 ml) sake
2 tablespoons soft brown sugar
3 teaspoons five-spice powder
1 teaspoon sea salt flakes
4 fillet steaks (200 g each)
600 g orange sweet potato, chopped
1 tablespoon butter
1/3 cup (90 g) sour cream
2 cloves garlic, crushed
1 teaspoon ground ginger
1 tablespoon peanut oil
2 teaspoons butter, for pan-frying, extra
1 teaspoon finely chopped fresh ginger
1 clove garlic, crushed, extra
100 g shiitake mushrooms, sliced
100 g shimeji mushrooms, pulled apart
100 g enoki mushrooms, trimmed
toasted sesame seeds, to serve

1 Place the soy sauce, mirin, sake and sugar in a small saucepan and boil over high heat for 5 minutes, or until reduced and thickened slightly. Remove from the heat and cover.
2 Rub the combined five-spice powder and sea salt flakes into the steaks.
3 Boil the orange sweet potato for 12 minutes, or until soft. Drain well, then add the butter, sour cream, garlic and ground ginger and mash together until smooth and creamy. Season, cover and keep warm.
4 Heat the oil in a large frying pan over high heat. When very hot, cook the steaks for 4–5 minutes each side for a medium–rare result, or until done to your liking. Remove from the pan, cover with foil and rest for 10 minutes.
5 Melt the extra butter in a frying pan over medium heat until just sizzling, then stir in the fresh ginger and extra garlic. Add the shiitake and shimeji mushrooms and stir for 3 minutes, or until wilted. Add the enoki, remove from the heat, cover and keep warm. Gently reheat the sauce and mashed sweet potato.
6 To serve, dollop mash on four plates, sit a steak on top, then spoon on the sauce. Top with mushrooms, sprinkle with sesame seeds and serve.

NUTRITION PER SERVE
Protein 47 g; Fat 28 g; Carbohydrate 13 g; Dietary Fibre 2.5 g; Cholesterol 180 mg; 2105 kJ (505 cal)

Boil until the sauce has reduced and thickened slightly.

Cook the mushrooms, stirring, until they are wilted.

DESSERTS

LEMON SHORTBREADS WITH MANGO CREAM

Preparation time: 40 minutes + 2 hours 35 minutes cooling
Total cooking time: 45 minutes
Serves 4

100 g unsalted butter, softened
3/4 cup (90 g) pure icing sugar
1 egg yolk
1/2 teaspoon vanilla essence
2 teaspoons grated lemon rind
1 teaspoon lemon juice
1 1/4 cups (155 g) plain flour
1 mango, cut into slices
sifted icing sugar, to serve

Mango cream
1/2 cup (125 ml) thick cream
3 egg yolks
1/4 cup (60 g) caster sugar
1/2 cup (135 g) fresh mango purée
1/3 cup (80 ml) cream, whipped

Mango sauce
1 mango
1 tablespoon caster sugar
1 tablespoon lemon juice

1 Cream the butter and sifted icing sugar until light, then add the egg yolk, vanilla essence, lemon rind and lemon juice. Sift in the flour and gently fold it into the mixture. Knead gently until the dough comes together. Cover the dough in plastic wrap and refrigerate for 2 hours.

2 Meanwhile, to make the mango cream, warm the thick cream in a small saucepan. Place the egg yolks and sugar in a heatproof bowl and whisk, then stir in the warmed cream. Place the bowl over a saucepan of simmering water, making sure the water does not touch the bowl. Stir over simmering water for 25–30 minutes, or until thick. Cool, stir in the mango purée, then fold in the whipped cream.

3 Preheat the oven to slow 150°C (300°F/Gas 2) and lightly grease a baking tray. Roll the dough out between two sheets of baking paper to 5 mm thick. Using a round 7 cm fluted cutter, cut out eight rounds, put on the tray and bake for 12–14 minutes, or until golden. Cool slightly on the tray before transferring to a wire rack.

4 To make the mango sauce, purée the mango flesh, sugar and lemon juice in a food processor or blender. Strain through a fine sieve or muslin.

5 To assemble, place one shortbread on a plate and add a dollop of mango cream, then a few mango slices. Follow with more mango cream and top with another biscuit. Dust with icing sugar and drizzle mango sauce onto the plate. Repeat, making three more serves.

NUTRITION PER SERVE
Protein 9 g; Fat 48 g; Carbohydrate 90 g; Dietary Fibre 3 g; Cholesterol 311 mg; 3430 kJ (820 cal)

Stir the custard over simmering water until it is very thick.

Cut out eight rounds from the dough with a 7 cm fluted cutter.

COFFEE CREAM PAVLOVA ROLL

Preparation time: 30 minutes + cooling time
Total cooking time: 30 minutes
Serves 6–8

Meringue
4 egg whites, at room temperature
3/4 cup (185 g) caster sugar
1 teaspoon vanilla essence
2 teaspoons white vinegar
2 teaspoons cornflour
1/3 cup (30 g) flaked almonds
1 tablespoon caster sugar, to sprinkle, extra

Toffee praline
1/3 cup (30 g) flaked almonds
1 1/3 cups (340 g) caster sugar

Coffee cream
1/2 cup (125 ml) cream
4–5 tablespoons very strong cold black coffee
2 tablespoons icing sugar
250 g mascarpone

1 Preheat the oven to warm 160°C (315°F/Gas 2–3). Lightly grease a 30 x 25 cm swiss roll tin and line the base and sides with baking paper. To make the meringue, beat the egg whites in a dry bowl until firm peaks form. Gradually beat in the sugar, beating for 5–8 minutes, or until the sugar has dissolved and the mixture is thick and glossy. Fold in the vanilla, vinegar and cornflour, then spread into the prepared tin and smooth the top. Sprinkle with almonds, then bake for 20 minutes, or until firm.

2 Meanwhile, to make the toffee praline, cover a baking tray with baking paper and sprinkle with almonds. Put the sugar and 1/2 cup (125 ml) water in a small saucepan and stir over low heat until the sugar dissolves. Bring to the boil and simmer without stirring until the toffee is dark golden—watch carefully as it can burn quickly. Pour over the almonds and leave until set. Break into small pieces or pulverise in a food processor. Set aside.

3 Put a large sheet of baking paper on a work surface and sprinkle with the extra caster sugar. Invert the meringue onto the paper so that the almonds are on the bottom. Peel off the lining paper and leave for 10 minutes.

4 To make the coffee cream, beat the cream in a small bowl until firm peaks form. Gently stir in the coffee, icing sugar and mascarpone and mix. Do not overbeat or it will curdle. Spread the meringue with the coffee cream and roll up firmly. Transfer to a plate. Sprinkle the toffee praline down the centre of the log, slice and serve.

NUTRITION PER SERVE (8)
Protein 6 g; Fat 21 g; Carbohydrate 48 g; Dietary Fibre 0.5 g; Cholesterol 52 mg; 1053 kJ (395 cal)

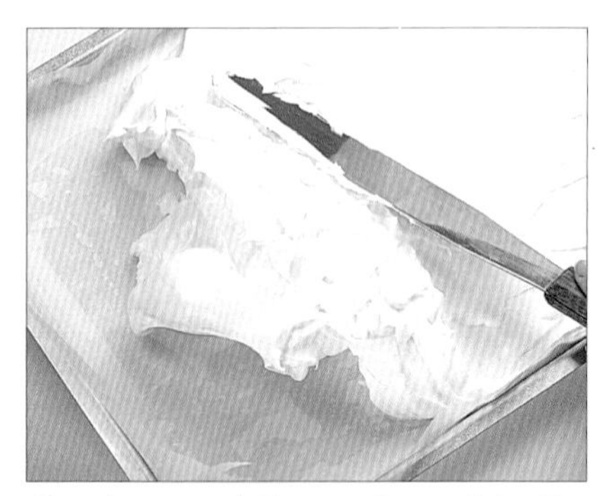

Evenly spread the meringue into the swiss roll tin and smooth the top.

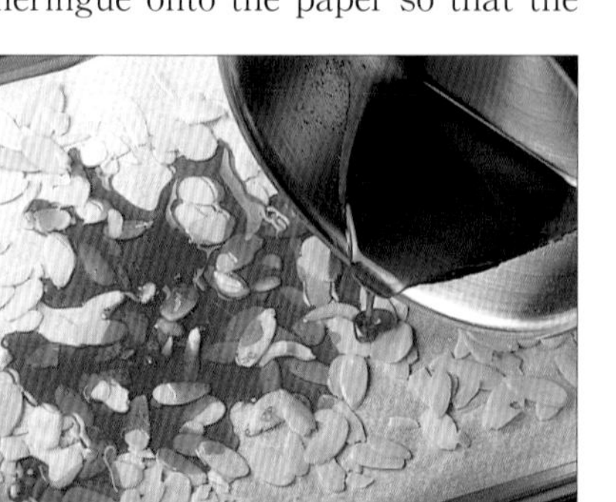

Pour the toffee over the almonds on the baking tray.

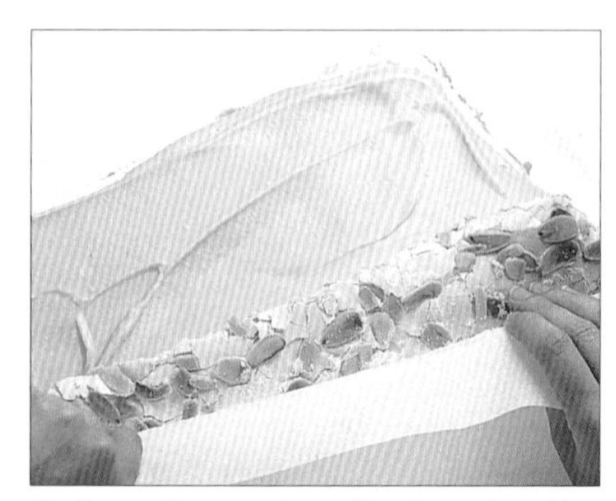

Roll up the pavlova firmly, using the baking paper to help you.

STICKY MAPLE PUDDINGS WITH NUTS

Preparation time: 40 minutes + 20 minutes standing
Total cooking time: 35 minutes
Serves 6

2 tablespoons soft brown sugar
60 g unsalted butter, cut into cubes
2/3 cup (170 ml) pure maple syrup
1/2 cup (70 g) roughly chopped macadamia nuts, toasted
1 cup (185 g) chopped pitted dates
1/2 teaspoon bicarbonate of soda
100 g unsalted butter, softened, extra
1/3 cup (60 g) soft brown sugar, extra
2 eggs, lightly beaten
1/2 cup (60 g) plain flour
1/2 cup (60 g) self-raising flour
1/4 teaspoon grated fresh nutmeg

Sauce
90 ml cream
2 tablespoons pure maple syrup
25 g unsalted butter
pinch grated fresh nutmeg

1 Lightly grease six Texan (large) muffin holes, then line the bases with baking paper. Place the sugar, butter and half the maple syrup in a small bowl and stir well. Spoon evenly into the bases of the prepared muffin holes, then evenly sprinkle with the macadamia nuts.
2 Preheat the oven to moderate 180°C (350°F/Gas 4). Put the dates in a saucepan, add the bicarbonate of soda and 3/4 cup (185 ml) boiling water and bring to the boil, then remove from the heat and leave for 15 minutes. Blend until smooth in a blender or food processor, then cool.
3 Beat the softened butter, extra sugar and remaining maple syrup in a small bowl with electric beaters until light and fluffy. Add the eggs one at a time, beating well after each addition—the mixture will appear curdled, but this is okay. Stir in the date mixture, then the combined sifted flours and nutmeg to form a smooth batter.
4 Spoon the mixture evenly into the prepared muffin holes, place a baking tray on the shelf under the muffin tray to catch any drips, and bake for 25–30 minutes, or until a skewer inserted into the centre comes out clean. Leave for 5 minutes. Invert the puddings onto a baking tray covered with baking paper. Any nut mixture stuck to the base of the muffin holes can be carefully replaced.
5 Meanwhile, to make the sauce, put the cream, maple syrup, butter and nutmeg in a saucepan, stir over low heat until the butter has dissolved, then simmer for 5 minutes, or until thickened slightly. Cool until just warm.
6 To serve, place a pudding in each serving bowl and spoon sauce all around. Serve with cream.

NUTRITION PER SERVE
Protein 6 g; Fat 40 g; Carbohydrate 89 g; Dietary Fibre 4.5 g; Cholesterol 149 mg; 2998 kJ (716 cal)

Stir in the date mixture and sifted flours until a smooth batter forms.

Simmer the maple sauce until it thickens slightly.

STRAWBERRY AND MASCARPONE TART

Preparation time: 45 minutes + 45 minutes refrigeration
Total cooking time: 30 minutes
Serves 6

Pastry
1 1/2 cups (185 g) plain flour
125 g unsalted butter, chilled and cut into cubes
1/3 cup (80 ml) iced water

Filling
500 g strawberries, hulled and halved
2 teaspoons vanilla essence
50 ml Drambuie
1/3 cup (60 g) soft brown sugar
250 g mascarpone
300 ml thick cream
2 teaspoons orange zest

1 Sift the flour into a large bowl and add the butter. Rub the butter into the flour with your fingertips until it resembles fine breadcrumbs. Make a well in the centre and add almost all the water and mix with a flat-bladed knife, using a cutting action, until the mixture comes together in beads, adding the remaining water if needed. Gently gather the dough together and lift out onto a lightly floured surface.

2 Roll the dough out between two sheets of baking paper until large enough to line the base and side of a lightly greased 22 cm (3.5 cm deep) loose-bottomed flan tin. Ease the pastry into the tin and trim the edge, then chill for 15 minutes. Preheat the oven to moderately hot 200°C (400°F/ Gas 6) and heat a baking tray.

3 Line the pastry with a sheet of baking paper and pour in some baking beads or rice, then bake on the heated baking tray for 15 minutes. Remove the paper and beads and bake for 10–15 minutes, or until dry and golden. Cool completely.

4 Meanwhile, place the strawberries, vanilla, Drambuie and 1 tablespoon of the brown sugar in a bowl and mix well. Place the mascarpone, cream, zest and remaining brown sugar in another bowl and mix. Cover both bowls and refrigerate for 30 minutes, tossing the strawberries once or twice.

5 Whip half the mascarpone cream until firm, then evenly spoon it into the tart shell. Drain the strawberries, reserving the liquid. Pile the strawberries onto the tart. Serve wedges of the tart with a drizzling of the reserved liquid and a dollop of the remaining mascarpone cream.

NUTRITION PER SERVE
Protein 9.5 g; Fat 53 g; Carbohydrate 37 g; Dietary Fibre 3 g; Cholesterol 162 mg; 2729 kJ (652 cal)

Mix with a flat-bladed knife until the mixture comes together in beads.

Remove the paper and baking beads from the pastry shell.

ALMOND TUILES AND CHERRY CONFIT STACK WITH ICE CREAM

Preparation time: 40 minutes + cooling time + 5 hours freezing
Total cooking time: 1 hour
Serves 4

Ice cream
300 g sour cream
1 cup (250 ml) cream
1 vanilla bean, split lengthways
5 egg yolks
1/2 cup (125 g) caster sugar

Cherry confit
3 x 425 g cans pitted black cherries
1/2 cup (125 g) caster sugar
1 vanilla bean, split lengthways
1 cinnamon stick
2 star anise

Almond tuiles
2 egg whites
1/2 cup (60 g) icing sugar
1/2 cup (60 g) plain flour, sifted
100 g flaked almonds
40 g unsalted butter, melted
1/4 teaspoon ground cinnamon

1 To make the ice cream, place the sour cream, cream and vanilla bean in a saucepan and stir over low heat until heated through.
2 Whisk the egg yolks and sugar in a bowl until pale and thick. Strain the cream mixture through a sieve into the egg mixture and whisk well. Return to a clean saucepan and stir constantly over low heat for 5 minutes, or until it thickens slightly and coats the back of a spoon—do not boil or it will curdle. Pour into a bowl, cover with plastic wrap and cool.
3 When the mixture has cooled, pour it into a shallow metal tin, cover with plastic wrap and freeze for 2 hours, or until almost set. Scoop into a chilled bowl and beat with electric beaters until smooth. Return to the tin and refreeze for 1 hour. Repeat twice more or freeze in an ice-cream maker, according to the manufacturer's instructions.
4 To make the confit, drain the cherries, reserving 2/3 cup (160 ml) of the syrup. Place all the ingredients and reserved liquid in a saucepan and simmer, stirring occasionally, for 25 minutes, or until the sugar has dissolved and the confit is thick and syrupy. Remove from the heat. Cool.
5 Preheat the oven to moderate 180°C (350°F/Gas 4). To make the tuiles, lightly grease two baking trays. Mark six 10 cm circles on a sheet of baking paper big enough to fit a baking tray. Repeat with another sheet. Place the sheets, pencil-side-down, on the trays. Whisk the egg whites and icing sugar in a bowl until well combined. Mix in the flour, almonds, butter and cinnamon. Spread level tablespoons of the mixture onto the marked circles. Bake one tray at a time for 8–10 minutes, or until lightly golden around the edges. Cool for 30 seconds on the tray before transferring to a wire rack to cool completely.
6 To serve, place one tuile on each plate and top with a little of the confit. Repeat, then finish with a third tuile. Dust with icing sugar and serve with a scoop of the ice cream. Serve immediately.

NUTRITION PER SERVE
Protein 17 g; Fat 85 g; Carbohydrate 148 g; Dietary Fibre 8 g; Cholesterol 432 mg; 5838 kJ (1395 cal)

Stir the custard until it is thick enough to coat the back of a spoon.

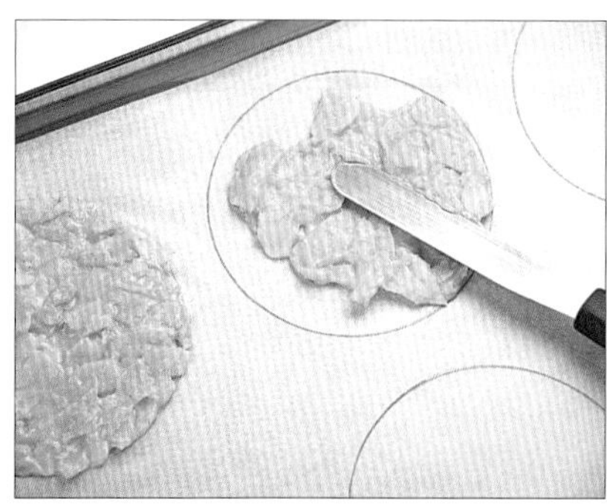

Spread level tablespoons of the tuile mixture onto the marked circles.

DARK CHOCOLATE AND MALT ICE CREAM WITH HAZELNUT MERINGUES

Preparation time: 35 minutes + cooling time + 6 hours freezing
Total cooking time: 1 hour 30 minutes
Serves 6

8 egg yolks
1/2 cup (125 g) caster sugar
1/3 cup (40 g) malted milk powder
2 cups (500 ml) cream
1 cup (250 ml) milk
1 vanilla bean, split lengthways
100 g dark chocolate, melted

Meringues
3 egg whites
170 g caster sugar
1/4 teaspoon vanilla essence
1/2 cup (60 g) toasted, skinned and finely chopped hazelnuts

1 Place the egg yolks in a large non-metallic bowl and gradually whisk in the sugar with a whisk until the sugar has dissolved and the mixture is thick and pale. (Do not use electric beaters or they will incorporate too much air.)
2 Divide the mixture into two smaller bowls and add the malt to one.
3 Combine the cream and milk in a saucepan. Scrape the seeds from the vanilla bean into the pan and add the pod. Slowly bring to the boil over medium heat. Remove the pod, then whisk half the mixture into each bowl.
4 Transfer all of the malt-flavoured custard to a small, clean saucepan and cook over low heat, stirring constantly, for about 20 minutes, or until thick and it coats the back of a spoon. Remove from the heat, strain into a bowl, cover with plastic wrap and cool completely. Repeat with the plain custard, stirring the melted chocolate into the strained mixture.
5 Pour the cooled malt custard into a shallow metal tin, cover with plastic wrap and freeze for 2 hours, or until almost set. Scoop into a chilled bowl and beat with electric beaters until smooth. Return to the tin and refreeze for 1 hour. Repeat this process twice or freeze in an ice-cream maker according to the manufacturer's instructions, until frozen but still spreadable. Smooth the malt ice cream into the base of six 2/3 cup (170 ml) dariole moulds or ramekins and freeze. Repeat the freezing and churning process with the chocolate custard, then spread over the frozen malt ice cream. Freeze until completely frozen.
6 To make the meringues, preheat the oven to very slow 140°C (275°F/ Gas 1). Place the egg whites in a large clean, dry bowl and whisk until stiff. Gradually add the sugar, whisking well after each addition until stiff and glossy; add the vanilla essence with the final portion of sugar.
7 Gently fold the hazelnuts into the meringue mixture, then spoon into a piping bag with a 1 cm plain nozzle. Line a baking tray with baking paper and pipe six large meringue spirals onto the paper, starting from the centre and working out. Bake the meringues for 1 hour, or until dry. Cool on a wire rack. Store in an airtight container. To serve, briefly dip the bases of the ice cream moulds into warm water, run a flat-bladed knife around the inside edge and unmould onto a large plate. Top with the meringues.

NUTRITION PER SERVE
Protein 9 g; Fat 36 g; Carbohydrate 65 g; Dietary Fibre 1 g; Cholesterol 295 mg; 2516 kJ (600 cal)

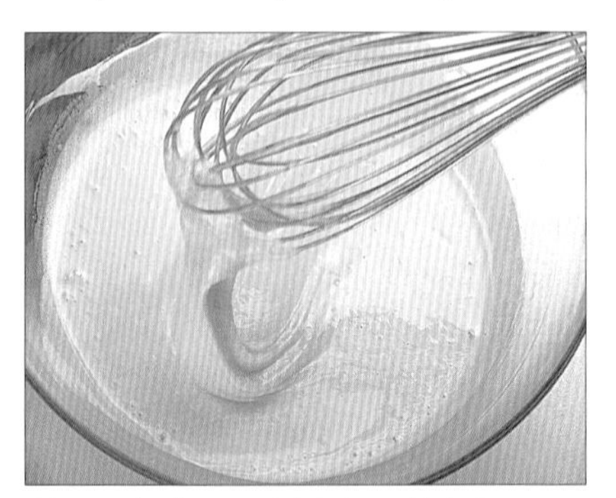

Use a balloon whisk to whisk the egg yolk mixture until thick and pale.

Scrape the seeds from the halved vanilla bean.

Stir the custard until it thickens and coats the back of a spoon.

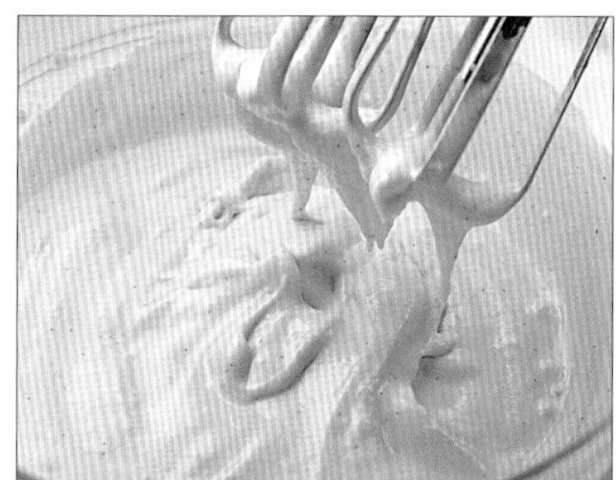

Beat the malt custard with electric beaters until smooth.

Spoon the chocolate custard over the frozen malt ice cream layer.

Pipe the hazelnut meringue mixture into six large spirals.

PISTACHIO CREME BRULEE

Preparation time: 25 minutes + 10 minutes standing + 6 hours refrigeration
Total cooking time: 1 hour 10 minutes
Serves 6

2 cups (500 ml) cream
1/4 cup (35 g) finely chopped pistachios
1/2 vanilla bean, halved lengthways
1/2 teaspoon grated orange rind
100 g caster sugar
5 egg yolks
1–3 tablespoons caster sugar, extra
pistachio biscotti, to serve

1 Preheat the oven to very slow 140°C (275°F/Gas 1). Place the cream, pistachios, vanilla bean, orange rind and half the sugar in a saucepan over medium heat and stir to dissolve the sugar, then slowly bring to the boil. Remove from the heat and leave to infuse for 10 minutes.

2 Whisk the egg yolks and remaining sugar together in a bowl. Strain the cream mixture into a jug, then add to the egg mixture, stirring continuously.

3 Ladle the custard into six 1/2 cup (125 ml) ramekins and place in a baking tin. Carefully pour in enough cold water to come halfway up the side of the ramekins, then place in the oven and cook for 1 hour, or until the custard has set and is only just wobbly.

4 Remove from the oven and place the ramekins on a wire rack to cool, then refrigerate for 4 hours.

5 Preheat the grill to very hot. Sprinkle 1–2 teaspoons of the extra sugar over the top of each brulée. Place the brulées in a roasting tin full of ice, then place the tin under the grill for 4 minutes, or until the tops of the brulées have melted and caramelised. Remove the ramekins from the roasting tin and dry around the outside edges with a tea towel.

6 Refrigerate for 1–2 hours but not more than 3 hours (if you keep them in the fridge any longer, the toffee will start to go sticky and lose its crunch). Serve with a couple of pieces of pistachio biscotti and some fresh fruit.

NUTRITION PER SERVE
Protein 5 g; Fat 43 g; Carbohydrate 25 g; Dietary Fibre 0.5 g; Cholesterol 262 mg; 2053 kJ (490 cal)

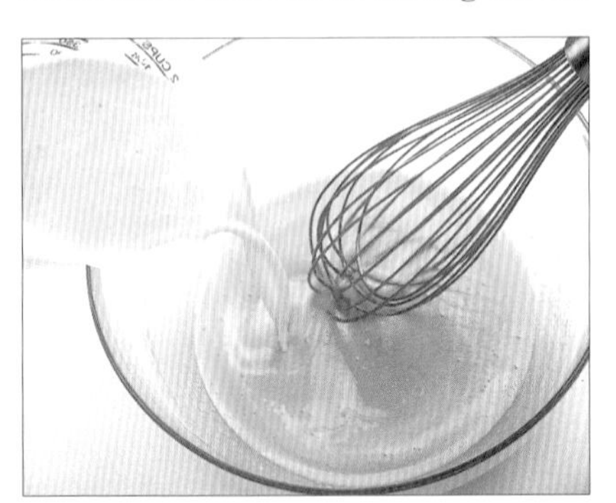

Pour the strained cream mixture into the bowl with the egg yolk mixture.

Bake the custard until it is set and only just wobbly.

Grill the custards until the sugar on the top melts and caramelises.

BERRY RICOTTA CREAM TARTLETS

Preparation time: 1 hour + 1 hour refrigeration
Total cooking time: 40 minutes
Serves 6

Pastry
1 1/2 cups (185 g) plain flour
1/2 cup (95 g) ground almonds
1/3 cup (40 g) icing sugar
125 g unsalted butter, chopped
1 egg, lightly beaten

Filling
200 g ricotta
1 teaspoon vanilla essence
2 eggs
2/3 cup (160 g) caster sugar
1/2 cup (125 ml) cream
1/2 cup (60 g) raspberries
1/2 cup (80 g) blueberries
icing sugar, to dust

1 Sift the flour into a large bowl, then add the almonds and icing sugar. Rub the butter into the flour with your fingertips until it resembles fine breadcrumbs. Make a well in the centre and add the egg and mix with a flat-bladed knife, using a cutting action, until the mixture comes together in beads. Gently gather the dough together and lift out onto a lightly floured work surface. Press together into a ball, cover with plastic wrap and refrigerate for 30 minutes.
2 Grease six 8 cm (3 cm deep) loose-bottomed tart tins. Divide the pastry into six and roll each piece out between two sheets of baking paper to fit the base and side of the tins. Ease the pastry into the tins, gently press into shape and trim the edges. Prick the bases with a fork, then refrigerate for 30 minutes. Preheat the oven to moderate 180°C (350°F/Gas 4).

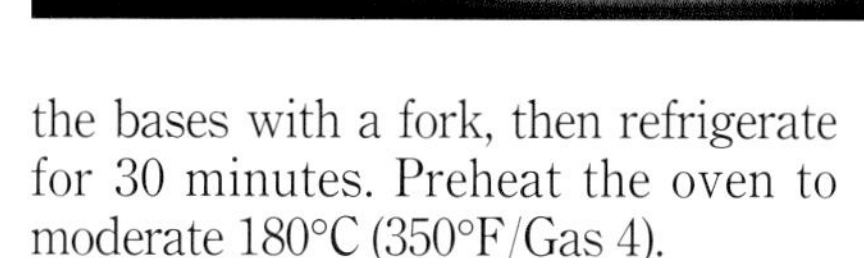

3 Line the pastry with a sheet of crumpled baking paper and spread with a layer of baking beads or (uncooked) rice. Bake for 8–10 minutes. Remove the paper and beads.
4 Meanwhile, process the ricotta, vanilla, eggs, sugar and cream in a food processor until smooth.
5 Divide the berries and filling among the tarts and bake for 25–30 minutes, or until the filling is just set—the top should be soft but not too wobbly. Cool. Dust with icing sugar and serve.

NUTRITION PER SERVE

Protein 14 g; Fat 42 g; Carbohydrate 62 g; Dietary Fibre 3.5 g; Cholesterol 187 mg; 2780 kJ (665 cal)

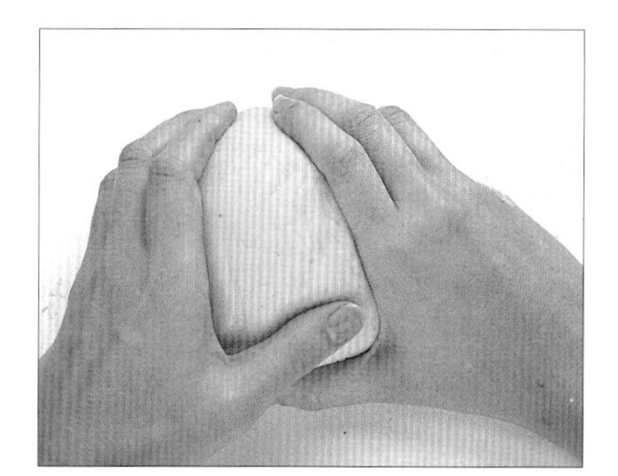

Gently gather the dough together and press into a ball.

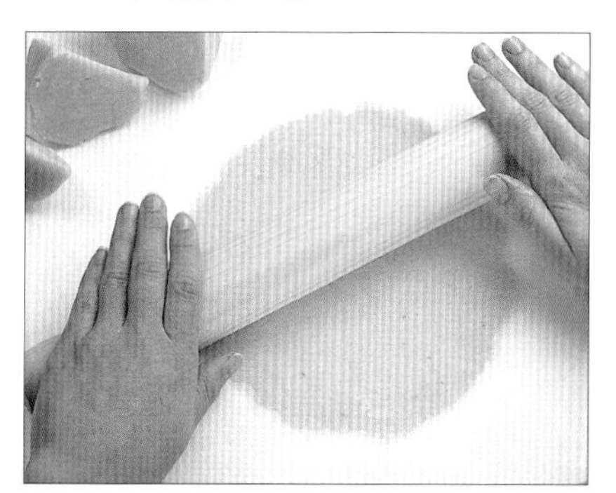

Roll the pastry between two sheets of baking paper.

Pour the filling over the berries in each pastry case.

ROASTED PINEAPPLE GRATIN

Preparation time: 15 minutes
Total cooking time: 15 minutes
Serves 4

800 g ripe pineapple, cut into 1.5 cm cubes
1/4 cup (60 ml) dark rum
2 tablespoons unsalted butter
1 teaspoon vanilla essence
1/4 cup (45 g) soft brown sugar
1/2 teaspoon ground ginger
300 g sour cream
1/4 cup (60 ml) cream
1 teaspoon finely grated lemon rind
1/2 cup (95 g) soft brown sugar, to sprinkle, extra

1 Place the pineapple, rum, butter, vanilla, sugar and ginger in a large saucepan and cook, stirring occasionally, for 8–10 minutes, or until caramelised. Remove from the heat.
2 Divide the pineapple among four individual gratin dishes and allow it to cool slightly.
3 Combine the sour cream, cream and lemon rind in a bowl, then spoon evenly over the pineapple. Sprinkle the extra brown sugar over each gratin.
4 Cook the gratins under a hot grill for 4–5 minutes, or until the sugar has melted and caramelised. Take care not to burn them. Serve immediately.

NUTRITION PER SERVE
Protein 4 g; Fat 44 g; Carbohydrate 53 g; Dietary Fibre 4 g; Cholesterol 142 mg; 2686 kJ (624 cal)

Cook the pineapple cubes in a large saucepan until caramelised.

Evenly sprinkle the brown sugar over the top of each gratin.

Grill the gratins until the sugar has melted and caramelised.

CITRUS TART

Preparation time: 1 hour + 30 minutes refrigeration
Total cooking time: 1 hour 45 minutes
Serves 6–8

Pastry
1 cup (125 g) plain flour
75 g unsalted butter, softened
1 egg yolk
2 tablespoons icing sugar, sifted

Filling
3 eggs
2 egg yolks
3/4 cup (185 g) caster sugar
1/2 cup (125 ml) cream
3/4 cup (185 ml) lemon juice
1 1/2 tablespoons finely grated lemon rind
2 small lemons
2/3 cup (160 g) sugar

1 To make the pastry, sift the flour and a pinch of salt into a large bowl. Make a well in the centre and add the butter, egg yolk and icing sugar. Work together the butter, yolk and sugar with your fingertips, then slowly incorporate the flour. Bring together into a ball—you may need to add a few drops of cold water. Flatten the ball slightly, cover with plastic wrap and refrigerate for 20 minutes.
2 Preheat the oven to moderately hot 200°C (400°F/Gas 6). Lightly grease a shallow 21 cm loose-bottomed flan tin.
3 Roll the pastry out between two sheets of baking paper to about 3 mm thick to fit the base and side of the tin. Trim the edge. Chill for 10 minutes. Line the pastry with crumpled baking paper, fill with baking beads or rice and bake for 10 minutes, or until cooked. Remove the paper and beads and bake for 6–8 minutes, or until the pastry looks dry all over. Cool the pastry and reduce the oven to slow 150°C (300°F/Gas 2).
4 Whisk the eggs, yolks and sugar together, add the cream and juice and mix well. Strain into a jug and add the rind. Place the flan tin on a baking sheet on the middle shelf of the oven and carefully pour in the filling. Bake for 40 minutes, or until just set—it should wobble in the middle when the tin is firmly tapped. Cool before removing from the tin.
5 Wash and scrub the lemons well. Slice very thinly (to about 2 mm). Combine the sugar and 200 ml water in a small frying pan and stir over low heat until the sugar has dissolved. Add the lemon slices and simmer over low heat for 40 minutes, or until the peel is very tender and the pith looks transparent. Lift out of the syrup and drain on baking paper. If serving the tart immediately, cover the surface with the lemon slices. If not, keep the slices covered and decorate the tart when ready to serve. Serve with whipped cream, if desired.

NUTRITION PER SERVE (8)
Protein 5.5 g; Fat 18 g; Carbohydrate 60 g; Dietary Fibre 1 g; Cholesterol 180 mg; 1766 kJ (422 cal)

Work the butter, yolk and sugar together, then add the flour.

Bake the tart until the citrus filling is just set.

Simmer the peel until it is very tender and the pith is transparent.

FLOURLESS CHOCOLATE CAKE

Preparation time: 1 hour + overnight refrigeration
Total cooking time: 1 hour 15 minutes
Serves 10

500 g good-quality dark chocolate, chopped
6 eggs
2 tablespoons Frangelico or brandy
1 1/2 cups (165 g) ground hazelnuts
1 cup (250 ml) cream, whipped
icing sugar, to dust
thick cream, to serve (optional)

1 Preheat the oven to slow 150°C (300°F/Gas 2). Grease a deep 20 cm round cake tin and line the base with baking paper.
2 Put the chocolate in a heatproof bowl. Half fill a saucepan with water and bring to the boil. Remove from the heat and sit the bowl over the pan, making sure it is not touching the water. Stir occasionally until the chocolate has melted.
3 Put the eggs in a large heatproof bowl and add the Frangelico. Place the bowl over a saucepan of barely simmering water on low heat, making sure the bowl does not touch the water. Beat the mixture with electric beaters on high speed for 7 minutes, or until light and foamy. Remove from the heat.
4 Using a metal spoon, quickly and lightly fold the melted chocolate and ground nuts into the egg mixture until just combined. Fold in the cream and pour into the prepared tin. Place the cake tin in a shallow roasting tin. Pour enough hot water into the roasting tin to come halfway up the side of the cake tin.
5 Bake the cake for 1 hour, or until just set. Remove the cake tin from the roasting tin and cool to room temperature. Cover with plastic wrap and refrigerate overnight.
6 Invert the cake onto a plate and remove the baking paper. Cut into slices, dust lightly with icing sugar and serve with thick cream.

NUTRITION PER SERVE
Protein 9 g; Fat 38 g; Carbohydrate 34 g; Dietary Fibre 2.5 g; Cholesterol 142 mg; 2135 kJ (510 cal)

Grease the cake tin and line the base with baking paper.

Beat the mixture over simmering water until light and foamy.

Gently fold the whipped cream into the chocolate nut mixture.

Place the cake tin in the roasting tin and bake until just set.

RASPBERRY BAVAROIS WITH BERRY SAUCE

Preparation time: 20 minutes + cooling time + 3 hours refrigeration
Total cooking time: 15 minutes
Serves 4

1/2 cup (125 ml) cream
200 g raspberries
1 tablespoon raspberry liqueur
1 teaspoon lemon juice
1/3 cup (90 g) caster sugar
1 egg, separated
1/2 cup (125 ml) milk
1/2 teaspoon vanilla essence
3 teaspoons gelatine
1 tablespoon unsalted butter
2 tablespoons soft brown sugar
1 tablespoon raspberry liqueur, extra
1 teaspoon lemon juice, extra
250 g strawberries, halved
150 g blueberries

1 Pour the cream into a bowl and beat until firm peaks form, then cover and refrigerate until needed. Process the raspberries, liqueur, lemon juice and 1/4 cup (60 g) of the caster sugar in a food processor until smooth. Strain through a sieve.

2 Put the egg yolk and remaining sugar in a bowl and whisk until pale and thickened, then whisk in the milk. Place the bowl on top of a small saucepan of simmering water and stir continuously for 5–10 minutes, or until the custard thickens slightly and coats the back of a spoon. Add the vanilla and remove from the heat.

3 Stir the gelatine into 1 tablespoon hot water until dissolved, then stir into the custard mixture. Cool to room temperature, then add the berry purée.

4 Whisk the egg white and a pinch of sugar together until firm peaks form, fold into the berry mixture, then slowly fold in the whipped cream. Pour into four lightly oiled 3/4 cup (185 ml) moulds. Chill for 3 hours, or until set.

5 To make the sauce, combine the butter, brown sugar, extra liqueur and lemon juice and 1 tablespoon water in a large frying pan, bring to the boil and cook for 1–2 minutes, or until thickened slightly. Add the berries and stir for 1–2 minutes, or until heated through, then remove from the heat and cool slightly.

6 Unmould the bavarois by running a knife around the edge, then turn out onto a plate. Spoon the sauce around the bavarois and serve.

NUTRITION PER SERVE
Protein 1 g; Fat 20 g; Carbohydrate 40 g; Dietary Fibre 5 g; Cholesterol 105 mg; 1534 kJ (366 cal)

Place the custard over simmering water and stir until slightly thickened.

Gently fold the egg whites into the berry custard mixture.

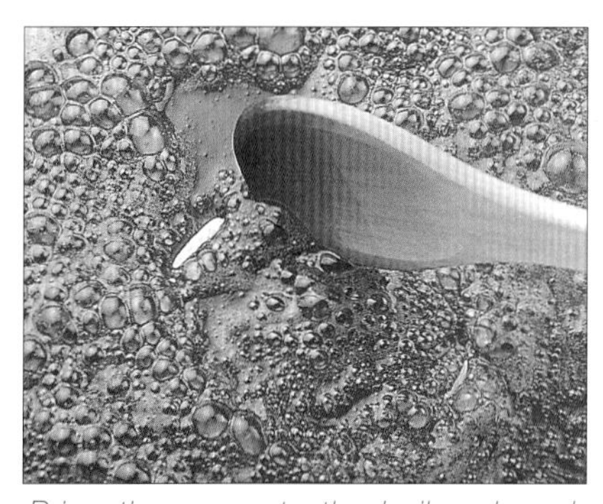

Bring the sauce to the boil and cook until it has thickened slightly.

PEARS IN SPICED WINE JELLY WITH FROZEN CARDAMOM PARFAIT

Preparation time: 50 minutes + 1 hour 20 minutes cooling + overnight freezing
Total cooking time: 40 minutes
Serves 6

Cardamom parfait
3/4 cup (185 ml) milk
1/4 teaspoon cardamom seeds
4 egg yolks
1/2 cup (125 g) caster sugar
1 cup (250 ml) cream

Pears in spiced wine jelly
6 corella pears or other small pears (about 90 g each)
1 cup (250 ml) red wine
1 cinnamon stick, broken
3 whole cloves
pinch cardamom seeds
1/2 cup (125 g) caster sugar
2 teaspoons gelatine

1 Lightly oil a 24 x 7 cm bar tin, then line the base and long sides with plastic wrap, allowing the excess to hang over the edges. Place the milk and cardamom seeds in a small saucepan, bring to the boil, then remove from the heat, cover and infuse for 10 minutes. Strain the mixture into a jug.
2 Beat the egg yolks and sugar in a small bowl with electric beaters until thick and pale, then gradually beat in the warm milk. Return the mixture to the saucepan and stir over medium heat for about 5 minutes, or until the mixture thickens slightly. Remove from the heat and pour into a bowl. Cover with plastic wrap, then refrigerate until cold.
3 Beat the cream in a bowl until soft peaks form, then gently fold into the cold custard mixture until combined. Pour into the prepared tin and fold the plastic gently over the top. Freeze overnight, or until firm.
4 Peel the pears, leaving the stems attached, then remove the core from the bottom with a melon baller. Check that the pears will fit in 1/2 cup (125 ml) dariole moulds. If the pears are a little too large, use the vegetable peeler to slice off some of the pear until it just fits—but take it slowly so that you don't cut off too much. Trim the bases so that the pears will sit flat in the moulds.
5 Place the wine, cinnamon stick, cloves, cardamom seeds, sugar and 3/4 cup (185 ml) water in a saucepan large enough to just fit the pears. Stir over medium heat until the sugar has dissolved. Add the pears to the syrup, cover and simmer for about 30 minutes, or until soft. Remove the pan from the heat and allow the pears to cool in the liquid.
6 Drain the pears well, reserving 1 cup (250 ml) of the liquid—if there is not enough, add water to make up the difference. Place the pears in six 1/2 cup (125 ml) dariole moulds.
7 Pour 1/4 cup (60 ml) of the poaching liquid into a small bowl and sprinkle the gelatine over it in an even layer. Leave until the gelatine is spongy: do not stir. Bring a small saucepan of water to the boil, remove from the heat and place the bowl with the gelatine mixture in the saucepan—the water should come halfway up the side of the bowl. Stir the gelatine until it has dissolved, then pour it into the remaining poaching liquid and stir together. Refrigerate, stirring occasionally, for 20 minutes until the mixture has set to the consistency of unbeaten egg whites.
8 Pour the mixture into the dariole moulds around the pears, standing the pears up as they fall over. Refrigerate for 1 hour, or until set. Check the fridge a couple of times and push the pears upright, if necessary.
9 Briefly dip the moulds in warm water and remove the jellied pears. Place on serving plates. Remove the cardamom parfait from the tin, remove the plastic wrap, then cut the parfait into eight slices. Place two slices slightly overlapping next to each of the pears. This dessert is best served immediately.

NUTRITION PER SERVE
Protein 5 g; Fat 22 g; Carbohydrate 53 g; Dietary Fibre 1.5 g; Cholesterol 180 mg; 1870 kJ (445 cal)

COOK'S FILE

NOTES: Dariole moulds are small bucket-shaped moulds.

If you can't find small pears, you can use regular pears instead. Pare the fruit down until it fits into the mould.

Line the tin with plastic wrap, allowing the excess to overhang the edges.

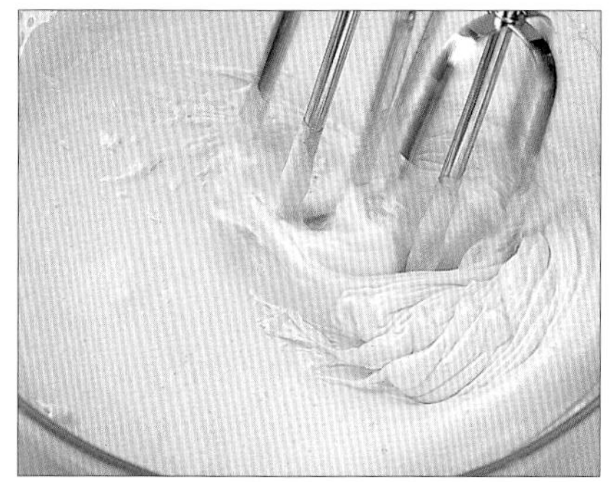

Beat the egg yolks and sugar until thick and pale.

Gently fold the whipped cream into the cold custard.

Sit the pears in the moulds, then pour the spiced wine mixture around them.

FROZEN ZABAGLIONE WITH MARSALA SAUCE

Preparation time: 15 minutes + 6 hours freezing
Total cooking time: 10 minutes
Serves 4

2/3 cup (170 ml) cream
3 egg yolks
1/2 teaspoon vanilla essence
3/4 cup (185 ml) Marsala
1/3 cup (90 g) caster sugar
1/3 cup (50 g) whole blanched almonds, toasted and chopped

1 Whip the cream to firm peaks, then cover and refrigerate until needed.

2 Place the egg yolks, vanilla, 1/2 cup (125 ml) of the Marsala and half of the sugar in a non-metallic bowl and whisk well.

3 Fill one third of a saucepan with water and bring to a simmer over medium heat. Sit the bowl on top of the saucepan, making sure the base of the bowl does not touch the water. Whisk continuously for 5 minutes, or until thick and foamy. The mixture should hold its form when you drizzle some from the whisk.

4 Remove from the heat and stand in a bowl of ice, whisking for 3 minutes, or until cool. Remove from the ice, then gently fold in the whipped cream and almonds. Carefully pour into four 1/2 cup (125 ml) dariole moulds or ramekins, cover with plastic wrap and freeze for 6 hours, or until firm.

5 Combine the remaining Marsala and sugar in a small saucepan and stir over low heat until the sugar dissolves. Bring just to the boil, then reduce the heat and simmer for 4–5 minutes, or until just syrupy—do not overcook or the syrup will harden when cool. Remove from the heat and set aside until needed

6 Briefly dip the moulds into warm water, then loosen with a knife. Turn out onto a plate and drizzle with sauce. Garnish with almonds, if desired.

NUTRITION PER SERVE
Protein 5.5 g; Fat 30 g; Carbohydrate 45 g; Dietary Fibre 1 g; Cholesterol 192 mg; 2190 kJ (523 cal)

Whisk the egg mixture continuously until thick and foamy.

Fold the whipped cream and chopped almonds into the egg mixture.

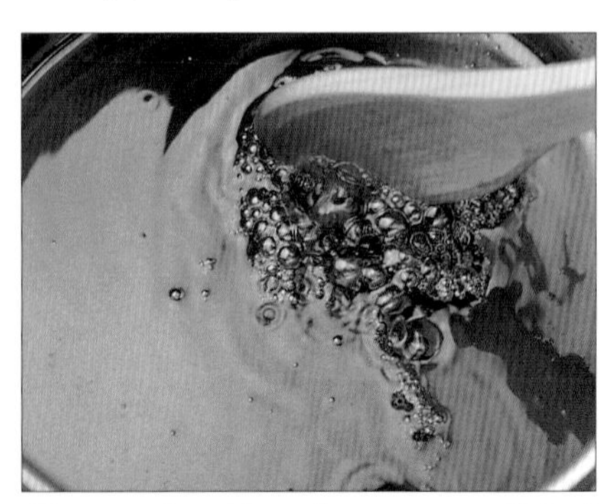

Simmer the Marsala sauce until just syrupy, then remove from the heat.

GRILLED FIGS WITH AMARETTO MASCARPONE

Preparation time: 10 minutes
Total cooking time: 15 minutes
Serves 4

- 1/4 cup (60 g) caster sugar
- 1/4 cup (60 ml) cream
- 1/2 teaspoon vanilla essence
- 1/2 cup (110 g) mascarpone
- 50 ml amaretto
- 1 1/2 tablespoons caster sugar, extra
- 1/4 cup (35 g) blanched almonds, finely chopped
- 1/2 teaspoon ground cinnamon
- 6 fresh figs, halved

1 Line a baking tray with foil. Place the caster sugar and 1/4 cup (60 ml) water in a small saucepan and stir over low heat until the sugar has dissolved, brushing down the side of the pan with a clean brush dipped in water if any crystals appear. Bring to the boil and cook, without stirring, for about 8 minutes, swirling occasionally until the mixture is golden. Quickly remove the pan from the heat and carefully pour in the cream, stirring constantly until smooth, then stir in the vanilla.

2 To make the amaretto mascarpone, place the mascarpone, amaretto and 2 teaspoons of the extra caster sugar in a bowl and mix together well.

3 Combine the chopped almonds, cinnamon and remaining caster sugar on a plate.

4 Press the cut side of each fig half into the almond mixture, then place, cut-side-up, onto the baking tray. Cook under a hot grill for 4–5 minutes, or until the sugar has caramelised and the almonds are nicely toasted—watch carefully to prevent burning.

5 Arrange three fig halves on each plate, place a dollop of the amaretto mascarpone to the side and drizzle with the sauce.

NUTRITION PER SERVE
Protein 5.5 g; Fat 22 g; Carbohydrate 27 g; Dietary Fibre 2 g; Cholesterol 52 mg; 1440 kJ (344 cal)

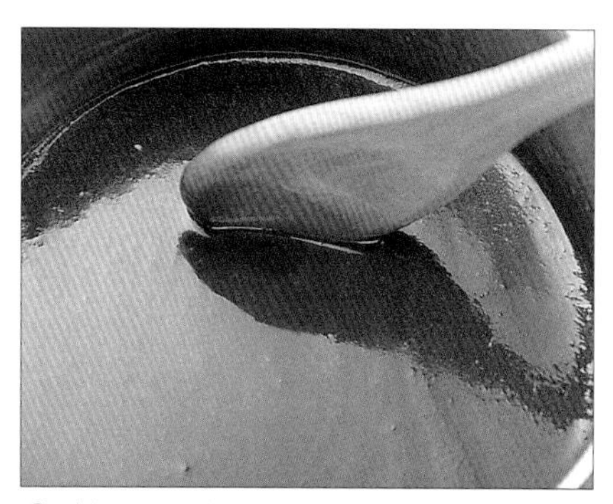

Swirl occasionally until the mixture is evenly golden.

Press the cut side of the figs into the almond mixture.

Cook the figs until the almonds are toasted but not burnt.

POACHED PEARS IN SAFFRON CITRUS SYRUP

Preparation time: 10 minutes
Total cooking time: 30 minutes
Serves 4

1 vanilla bean, split lengthways
1/2 teaspoon firmly packed saffron threads
3/4 cup (185 g) caster sugar
2 teaspoons grated lemon rind
4 pears, peeled
whipped cream, to serve (optional)
biscotti, to serve (optional)

1 Place the vanilla bean, saffron threads, sugar, lemon rind and 2 cups (500 ml) water in a large saucepan and mix together well. Heat, stirring, over low heat until the sugar has dissolved. Bring to the boil, then reduce to a gentle simmer.

2 Add the pears and cook, covered, for 12–15 minutes, or until tender when tested with a metal skewer. Turn the pears over with a slotted spoon halfway through cooking. Once cooked, remove from the syrup with a slotted spoon.

3 Remove the lid and allow the saffron citrus syrup to come to the boil. Cook for 8–10 minutes, or until the syrup has reduced by half and thickened slightly. Remove the vanilla bean and drizzle the syrup over the pears. Serve with whipped cream and a couple of pieces of biscotti.

NUTRITION PER SERVE
Protein 0.5 g; Fat 0 g; Carbohydrate 70 g; Dietary Fibre 4.5 g; Cholesterol 0 mg; 1155 kJ (276 cal)

COOK'S FILE

NOTE: Biscotti are available in a wide variety of flavours. You can buy biscotti at gourmet food stores, delicatessens and good supermarkets.

Stir the saffron citrus syrup until the sugar has dissolved.

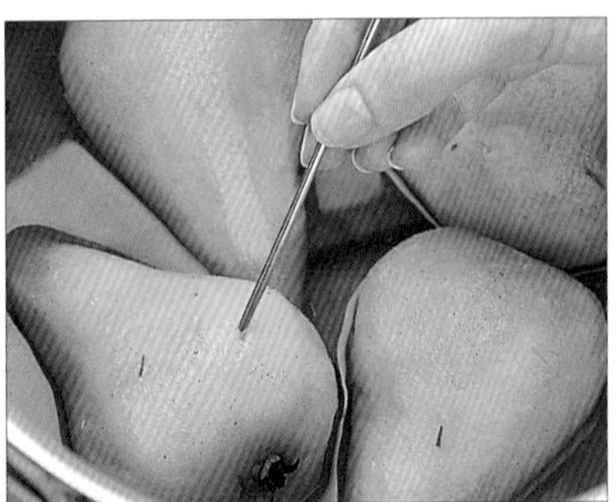

Cook the pears until tender when tested with a metal skewer.

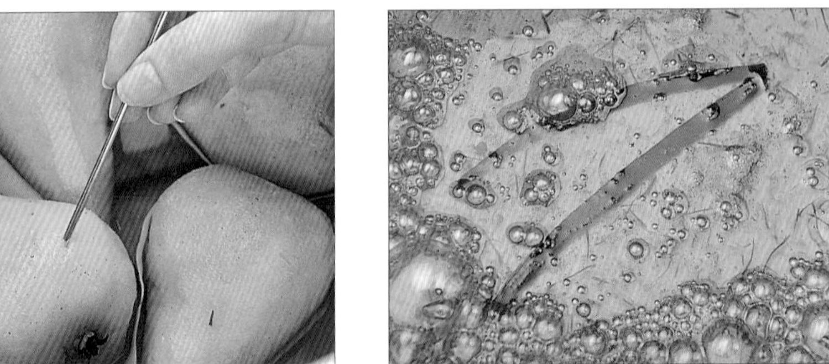

Bring the syrup to the boil and cook until slightly thickened.

WATERMELON AND VODKA GRANITA

Preparation time: 10 minutes + 5 hours freezing
Total cooking time: Nil
Serves 4–6

- 1 kg piece of watermelon, rind removed to give 600 g flesh
- 2 teaspoons lime juice
- 1/4 cup (60 g) caster sugar
- 1/4 cup (60 ml) citrus-flavoured vodka

1 Coarsely chop the watermelon, removing the seeds. Place the flesh in a food processor and add the lime juice and sugar. Process until smooth, then strain through a fine sieve. Stir in the vodka, then taste—if the watermelon is not very sweet, you may have to add a little more sugar.
2 Pour into a shallow 1.5 litre metal tin and freeze for about 1 hour, or until beginning to freeze around the edges. Scrape the frozen parts back into the mixture with a fork. Repeat every 30 minutes for about 4 hours, or until even ice crystals have formed.
3 Serve immediately or beat with a fork just before serving. To serve, scrape into dishes with a fork.

NUTRITION PER SERVE (6)
Protein 0.5 g; Fat 0 g; Carbohydrate 18 g; Dietary Fibre 1 g; Cholesterol 0 mg; 410 kJ (98 cal)

COOK'S FILE

SERVING SUGGESTION: A scoop of the granita in a shot glass with vodka is a hit at summer cocktail parties.
VARIATION: A tablespoon of finely chopped mint may be stirred through the mixture after straining the liquid.

Coarsely chop the watermelon flesh, removing the seeds.

Scrape the frozen parts around the edge back into the mixture.

Scrape the frozen parts back into the mixture until even ice crystals form.

UPSIDE-DOWN BANANA CAKE

Preparation time: 20 minutes
Total cooking time: 45 minutes
Serves 8

50 g unsalted butter, melted
1/3 cup (60 g) soft brown sugar
3–4 large ripe bananas, halved lengthways
125 g softened butter
1 1/4 cups (230 g) soft brown sugar, extra
2 eggs, lightly beaten
1 1/2 cups (185 g) self-raising flour
1 teaspoon baking powder
2 large ripe bananas, mashed, extra

1 Preheat the oven to moderate 180°C (350°F/Gas 4). Grease and line a 20 cm square cake tin, pour the melted butter over the base of the tin and sprinkle with the brown sugar. Arrange the bananas, cut-side-down, over the sugar.

2 Cream the butter and extra soft brown sugar until a light and fluffy mixture forms. Gradually add the eggs, beating well after each addition.

3 Sift the flour and baking powder into a bowl, then fold into the cake mixture with the mashed banana. Carefully spread into the cake tin. Bake for 45 minutes, or until a skewer comes out clean when inserted in the centre of the cake. Turn out while still warm. Serve the cake, banana-side-up, with cream or vanilla ice cream, if desired.

NUTRITION PER SERVE
Protein 5.5 g; Fat 20 g; Carbohydrate 70 g; Dietary Fibre 3 g; Cholesterol 100 mg; 1935 kJ (465 cal)

Arrange the bananas, cut-side-down, over the brown sugar.

Beat the butter and brown sugar until light and fluffy.

Fold the flour, baking powder and mashed banana into the mixture.

WARM APPLE 'BAKLAVA' WITH CINNAMON CREME ANGLAIS

Preparation time: 25 minutes
Total cooking time: 40 minutes
Serves 4

1 cup (250 ml) milk
2 cinnamon sticks
2 egg yolks
2 tablespoons caster sugar
3 Granny Smith apples, peeled, cored and cut into 1 cm dice
1 tablespoon lemon juice
2 tablespoons unsalted butter
2 tablespoons honey
1/4 teaspoon allspice
1/4 teaspoon ground ginger
1 teaspoon rosewater
2 tablespoons chopped toasted almonds
2 tablespoons chopped walnuts
2 tablespoons chopped pistachios
2 sheets frozen puff pastry, thawed
1 tablespoon unsalted butter, melted
1 tablespoon icing sugar
sliced pistachios, to garnish

1 Gently heat the milk and cinnamon sticks in a small saucepan and simmer for 5 minutes. Remove from the heat and infuse for about 5 minutes, then take out the cinnamon sticks.

2 Place the egg yolks and sugar in a small bowl and whisk well, then whisk in the milk until smooth. Transfer to a small saucepan and stir over low heat for 10 minutes, or until the mixture is thick enough to coat the back of a spoon. Remove from the heat, cover and keep warm.

3 Preheat the oven to moderately hot 200°C (400°F/Gas 6). Lightly grease two baking trays. Toss the apple in the lemon juice. Put the butter, honey, spices and rosewater in a frying pan and cook over medium heat for 1 minute, or until the butter bubbles. Add the apple and cook, stirring occasionally, for 10 minutes, or until the apple begins to caramelise. Stir in the nuts, then remove from the heat, cover and keep warm.

4 Lay the pastry sheets flat on a workbench, prick all over with a fork, then brush evenly with the melted butter. Sift the icing sugar over one of the sheets. Cut four 7 cm diamonds from each sheet, then carefully transfer to the baking trays. Bake for about 10 minutes, or until the pastry is crisp and golden. Reheat the apples gently if necessary.

5 To serve, divide the crème anglaise among four serving bowls and top with an unsugared pastry diamond. Divide the apple mixture among the pastry diamonds, then top with a sugared diamond. Garnish with pistachios and serve.

NUTRITION PER SERVE
Protein 13 g; Fat 40 g; Carbohydrate 70 g; Dietary Fibre 5 g; Cholesterol 125 mg; 2875 kJ (687 cal)

Stir until the mixture thickens enough to coat the back of a spoon.

Cook the apple in the butter mixture until it begins to caramelise.

Use a ruler to help you cut out eight 7 cm diamonds.

TUILE CONE WITH GINGER MOUSSE AND APRICOT SAUCE

Preparation time: 1 hour + refrigeration
Total cooking time: 40 minutes
Serves 8

60 g dried apricots, thinly sliced
1/2 vanilla bean
3/4 cup (185 ml) dessert wine
1/4 cup (60 g) caster sugar

Ginger mousse
1/4 cup (60 ml) green ginger wine
3 teaspoons gelatine
1 cup (250 ml) milk
3 egg yolks
1/3 cup (90 g) caster sugar
1 cup (250 ml) thick cream
1 1/2 tablespoons finely chopped glacé ginger

Tuile cones
40 g unsalted butter
1 tablespoon honey
1/3 cup (40 g) plain flour
1 egg white
1/4 cup (45 g) soft brown sugar
icing sugar, to dust

1 To make the sauce, cover the apricots with boiling water for 5 minutes, then drain. Cut the vanilla bean in half lengthways and scrape the seeds into a small saucepan. Add the pod, dessert wine and sugar. Stir over low heat until the sugar has dissolved. Simmer for 5 minutes, or until slightly syrupy, then remove from the heat and discard the pod.
2 To make the mousse, pour the wine into a small bowl and sprinkle with an even layer of gelatine. Leave until the gelatine is spongy—do not stir.
3 Boil the milk in a small saucepan, then remove from the heat. Beat the egg yolks and sugar in a small bowl with electric beaters until light and fluffy, then gradually beat in the hot milk. Return to the pan and stir over low heat for 5–8 minutes, or until it starts to thicken. Remove from the heat and pour into a large bowl. Add the gelatine mixture and stir until dissolved. Refrigerate, stirring occasionally, for 45 minutes, or until it reaches the consistency of unbeaten egg white. Fold in the cream and ginger, then return to the fridge.
4 Meanwhile, to make the tuiles, preheat the oven to moderate 180°C (350°F/Gas 4). Draw two 15 cm circles on a piece of baking paper large enough to cover a lightly greased baking tray. Put all the ingredients in a small bowl and beat with electric beaters for 2 minutes. Using a palette knife, spread 1 tablespoon of the mixture evenly over each circle.
5 Bake for 6 minutes, or until golden. Working quickly, trim a crescent off one side, then wrap firmly around a large metal horn mould, placing the point of the mould at the rounded edge of the tuile, opposite the trimmed edge (this will help it stand up when filled). Repeat with the remaining mixture until it is all used up—we have allowed more than eight in case any break.
6 Spoon the mousse into a piping bag fitted with a large plain nozzle (beat the mousse slightly if it has set). Pipe the mousse into the cones, and stand upright in the centre of a plate. Spoon some sauce and apricots around the base. Dust with icing sugar.

NUTRITION PER SERVE
Protein 5 g; Fat 20 g; Carbohydrate 32 g; Dietary Fibre 1 g; Cholesterol 126 mg; 1380 kJ (330 cal)

Simmer the apricot sauce over low heat until slightly syrupy.

Leave the gelatine on the wine until it is spongy—do not stir.

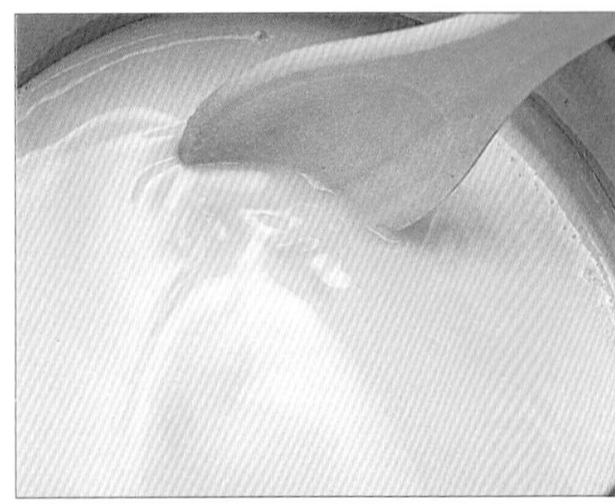

Stir the custard mixture over low heat until it starts to thicken.

Fold the thick cream and glacé ginger into the custard mixture.

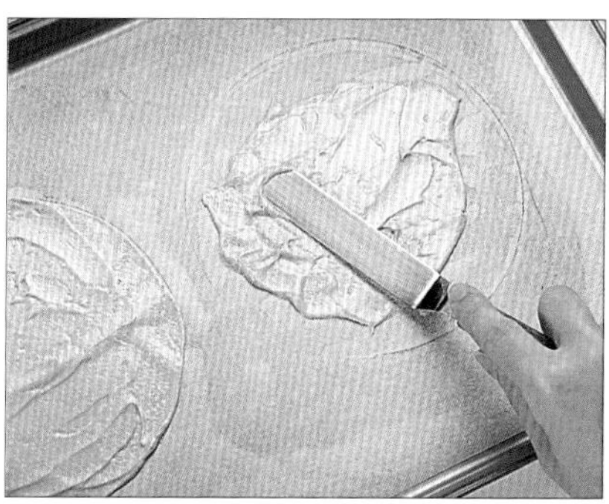

Using a palette knife, cover each circle with a layer of the tuile mixture.

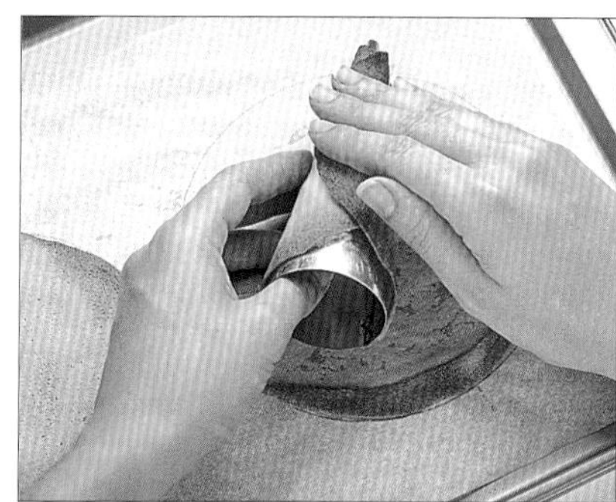

Trim off a small crescent, then wrap around a large metal horn mould.

BANANA TEMPURA WITH GREEN TEA ICE CREAM

Preparation time: 30 minutes + overnight refrigeration
Total cooking time: 25 minutes
Serves 4

Ice cream
1/3 cup (10 g) Japanese green tea leaves
2 cups (500 ml) milk
6 egg yolks
1/2 cup (125 g) caster sugar
2 cups (500 ml) cream

Banana tempura
oil, for deep-frying
1 egg
3/4 cup (185 ml) iced water
2/3 cup (85 g) tempura flour
4 small bananas, split in half lengthways and cut in half crossways
caster sugar, to sprinkle
warmed honey, to serve (optional)

1 Combine the tea leaves and the milk in a saucepan and bring to simmering point over low heat. Do not rush this step—the longer the milk takes to come to a simmer, the better the flavour. Set aside for 5 minutes before straining the liquid into a bowl.
2 Whisk the egg yolks and sugar in a heatproof bowl until thick and pale, then add the infused milk. Place the bowl over a saucepan of simmering water, making sure that the base of the bowl is not touching the water. Stir the custard until it is thick enough to coat the back of spoon, then remove from the heat and allow to cool slightly before adding the cream.
3 Pour the mixture into a metal tray and freeze for 1 1/2–2 hours, or until just frozen around the edges. Transfer the mixture to a chilled bowl, beat with electric beaters until thick and creamy, then return to the metal tray. Repeat the freezing and beating twice more. Transfer to a storage container, cover the surface with baking paper and freeze overnight. Alternatively, freeze in an ice-cream maker according to the manufacturer's instructions.
4 Heat the oil in a deep-fryer or heavy-based saucepan until a cube of bread browns in 20 seconds. Mix together the egg and water in a bowl, then stir in the tempura flour. Do not whisk the batter—it must be lumpy.
5 Dip the banana quarters into the batter and deep-fry a few at a time for about 2 minutes, or until crisp and golden. Drain on paper towels and sprinkle with caster sugar. Serve four pieces of banana with a scoop of ice cream. Drizzle with warmed honey.

NUTRITION PER SERVE
Protein 16 g; Fat 77 g; Carbohydrate 80 g; Dietary Fibre 3.5 g; Cholesterol 494 mg; 4413 kJ (1054 cal)

Whisk the egg yolks and sugar in a heatproof bowl until thick and pale.

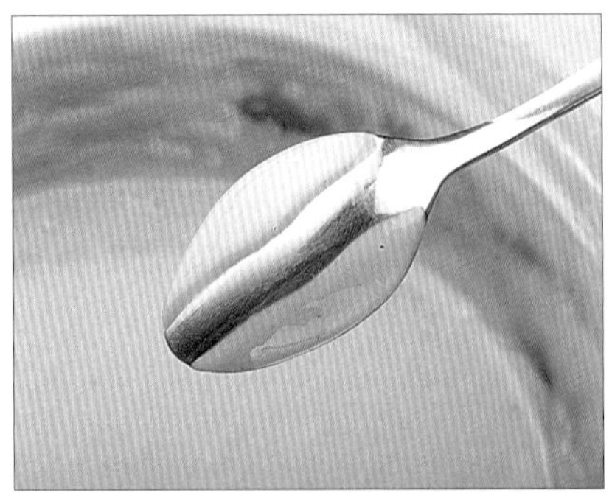

Stir the custard until it is thick enough to coat the back of a spoon.

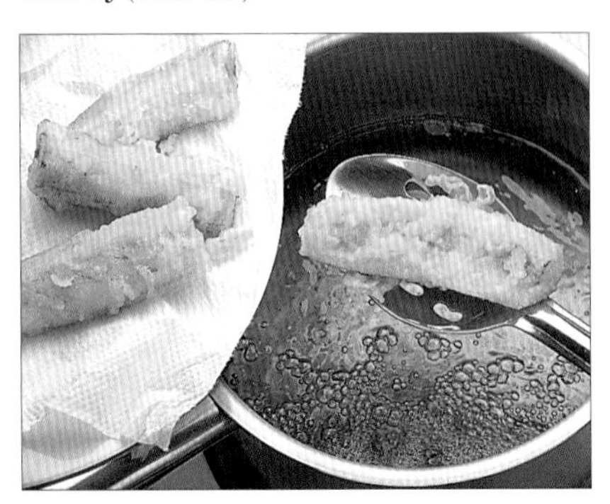

Deep-fry the bananas until crisp and golden, then drain on paper towels.

PASSIONFRUIT AND LEMON CUSTARD WITH LANGUES DES CHATS

Preparation time: 25 minutes + 1 hour 30 minutes cooling time
Total cooking time: 40 minutes
Serves 4

4 egg yolks
1/4 cup (60 g) caster sugar
75 ml milk
75 ml cream
25 ml seedless passionfruit pulp
50 ml lemon juice
icing sugar, to dust

Lemon langues des chats
60 g unsalted butter, softened slightly
1/2 cup (125 g) caster sugar
1/2 teaspoon finely grated lemon rind
2 egg whites
50 g plain flour

1 Preheat the oven to very slow 140°C (275°F/Gas 1). To make the custard, beat the egg yolks and sugar together, then mix in the milk, followed by the cream and finally the passionfruit pulp and lemon juice.
2 Divide the mixture among four 1/2 cup (125 ml) ramekins. Place the ramekins in a roasting tin and pour in enough warm water to come halfway up the side of the ramekins. Place the roasting tin in the oven and cook the custards for 30 minutes, or until set. Remove the ramekins from the water bath and cool on a wire rack before transferring them to the refrigerator. Refrigerate for at least 1 hour. Increase the oven to moderately hot 190°C (375°F/Gas 5).
3 Lightly grease two baking trays. To make the langues des chats, put the butter, sugar and lemon rind in a small bowl and beat together with a wooden spoon until pale and creamy. Add the egg whites and beat briefly. Sift the flour into the mixture and fold it in.
4 Transfer the mixture to a piping bag with a 1 cm wide, plain nozzle. Pipe the mixture into 8 cm long strips on the baking trays, squeezing a little harder at each end to achieve the traditional 'cat's tongue' shape and spacing them well apart to allow for spreading. Cook in the preheated oven for 5–7 minutes, or until the edges and base of the biscuits are lightly brown.
5 Remove the biscuits from the oven. After a couple of minutes, transfer the biscuits to a wire rack and cool completely. Dust the custards with a little icing sugar and serve each with two langues des chats.

NUTRITION PER SERVE
Protein 7 g; Fat 26 g; Carbohydrate 57 g; Dietary Fibre 0.5 g; Cholesterol 245 mg; 2012 kJ (480 cal)

Transfer the set custards from the roasting tin to a wire rack.

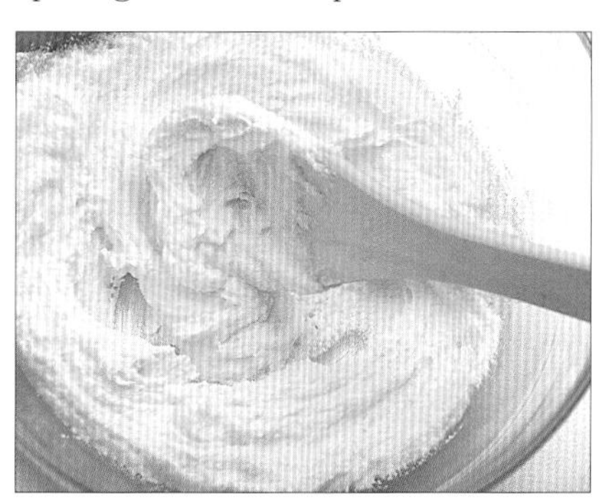

Beat the butter, sugar and lemon rind until pale and creamy.

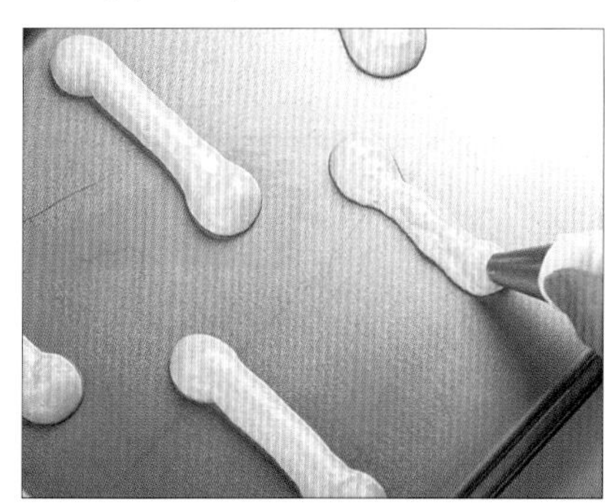

Pipe the mixture into 'cat's tongues', spacing them well apart.

MANGO PANNA COTTA

Preparation time: 30 minutes + 4 hours refrigeration
Total cooking time: 10 minutes
Serves 4

1 mango
2 teaspoons lime juice
3 1/2 sheets gelatine
1 vanilla bean
2 cups (500 ml) cream
1/3 cup (80 ml) milk
1/2 cup (125 g) caster sugar
1 mango, cut into small cubes, extra
1 teaspoon finely chopped fresh mint

1 Peel the mango, then roughly chop the flesh and place it in a food processor with the lime juice and process until smooth. Push the purée through a fine strainer into a bowl.
2 Soak the gelatine leaves in cold water for about 10 minutes.
3 Meanwhile, cut the vanilla bean in half lengthways, then scrape out the seeds. Place the vanilla seeds and pod, cream, milk and sugar in a saucepan and stir to dissolve the sugar, then simmer over medium heat, stirring occasionally, for 10 minutes. Remove from the heat and leave to infuse for 5 minutes, then strain into a clean bowl.
4 Remove the gelatine sheets from the water and squeeze out any excess moisture. Add the sheets to the cream mixture and stir until the gelatine has dissolved. Pour in the mango purée and mix together.
5 Pour the mixture into four lightly oiled 3/4 cup (185 ml) moulds, cover with plastic wrap and refrigerate for 4 hours, or until set. Meanwhile, combine the cubed mango with the mint, then cover and refrigerate until ready to serve.
6 To serve, quickly dip the moulds into a bowl of warm water, then loosen the panna cotta with a knife if necessary before carefully tipping out onto a plate. Serve topped with the mango and mint.

NUTRITION PER SERVE
Protein 7 g; Fat 55 g; Carbohydrate 55 g; Dietary Fibre 2 g; Cholesterol 173 mg; 3030 kJ (724 cal)

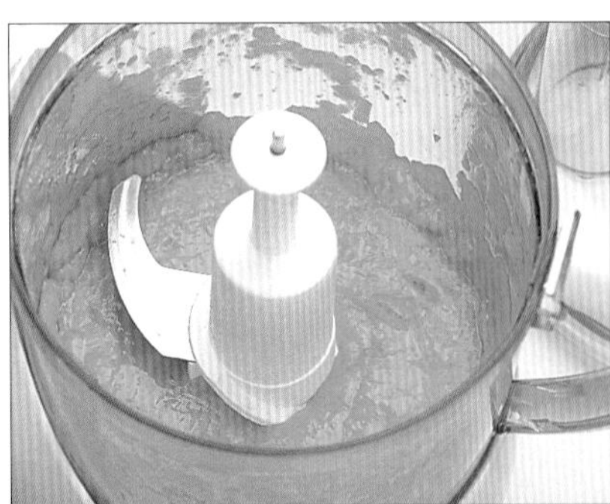

Blend the mango and lime juice in a food processor until smooth.

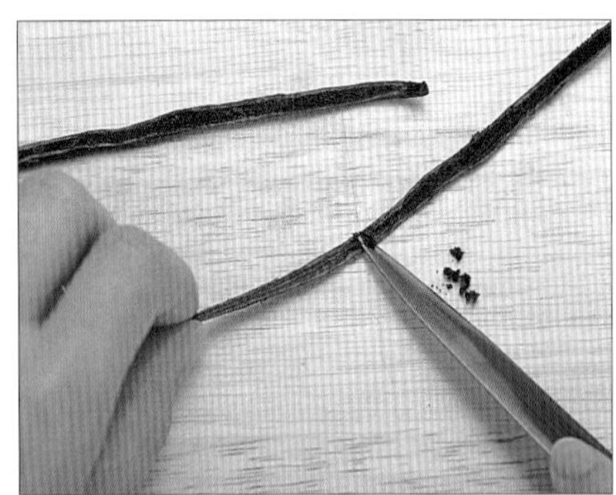

Cut the vanilla bean in half, then scrape out the seeds.

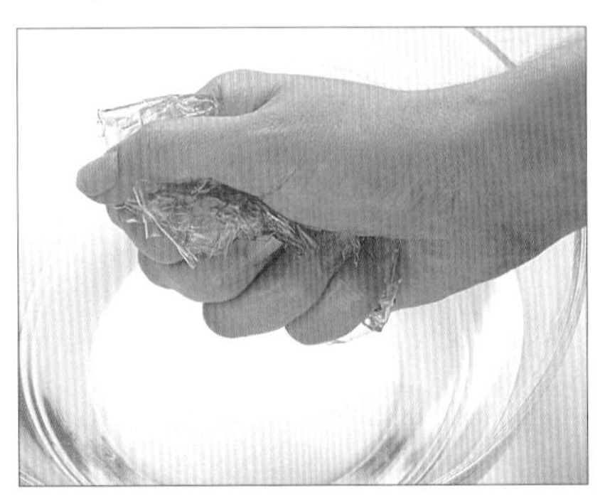

Squeeze out the excess moisture from the soaked gelatine sheets.

Cover the moulds with plastic wrap and refrigerate until set.

WHITE CHOCOLATE AND RASPBERRY CHEESECAKE

Preparation time: 40 minutes + cooling time
Total cooking time: 1 hour
Serves 8

375 g digestive biscuits, finely crushed
185 g unsalted butter, melted
2 cups (500 g) cream cheese, at room temperature
1/3 cup (90 g) caster sugar
4 eggs, lightly beaten
300 g sour cream
1 2/3 cups (250 g) white chocolate melts, melted
200 g raspberries
70 g white chocolate melts, melted, extra
raspberries, to garnish

Raspberry sauce
300 g fresh or frozen raspberries
1 tablespoon icing sugar

1 Grease a 23 cm round springform cake tin and line the base and side with baking paper. Place the biscuits and butter in a bowl and mix together. Press the mixture firmly into the base and side of the tin and refrigerate for 10 minutes. Preheat the oven to warm 160°C (315°F/Gas 2–3).

2 Beat the cream cheese and sugar together until smooth and creamy. Add the eggs gradually, beating well after each addition. Beat in the sour cream and the cooled white chocolate melts. Pour half the mixture into the chilled base and sprinkle with berries. Top with the remaining cream cheese mixture, then place on a baking tray and bake for 50–60 minutes, or until set. Cool to room temperature.

3 Meanwhile, place the extra melted chocolate in a piping bag with a 4 mm plain nozzle. Pipe decorative shapes onto baking paper. Set.

4 To make the raspberry sauce, put the raspberries and icing sugar in a food processor and process until smooth. Strain through a fine sieve.

5 Serve wedges of the cheesecake with a drizzle of sauce, some berries and decorated with chocolate shapes.

NUTRITION PER SERVE
Protein 16 g; Fat 78 g; Carbohydrate 74 g; Dietary Fibre 5 g; Cholesterol 276 mg; 4374 kJ (1045 cal)

Line the base and side of a round cake tin with baking paper.

Sprinkle the raspberries over half the cream cheese mixture.

Pipe the melted white chocolate into decorative shapes.

CARAMELISED APPLE MOUSSE

Preparation time: 20 minutes + 3 hours refrigeration
Total cooking time: 20 minutes
Serves 4

50 g unsalted butter
1/4 cup (60 g) caster sugar
2/3 cup (170 ml) cream
500 g green apples, peeled, cored and cut into thin wedges
2 eggs, separated

1 Place the butter and sugar in a frying pan and stir over low heat until the sugar has dissolved. Increase the heat to medium and cook until the mixture turns deeply golden, stirring frequently. Add 2 tablespoons of the cream and stir to remelt the caramel.
2 Add the apple wedges and cook, stirring frequently, over medium heat for 10–15 minutes, or until caramelised. Remove eight apple wedges and set aside to use as garnish.
3 Blend the remaining apples and caramel in a food processor until smooth. Transfer to a large bowl, then stir in the egg yolks and leave to cool.
4 Whisk the egg whites in a clean, dry bowl until soft peaks form, then fold into the cooled apple mixture.
5 Whip the remaining cream until firm peaks form and fold into the apple mixture. Pour into a 3 cup (750 ml) serving bowl or four 3/4 cup (185 ml) individual serving moulds. Refrigerate for 3 hours, or until firm. Serve with the reserved apple wedges.

NUTRITION PER SERVE
Protein 4.5 g; Fat 30 g; Carbohydrate 30 g; Dietary Fibre 2.5 g; Cholesterol 180 mg; 1699 kJ (405 cal)

Cook the apple wedges in the butter and sugar until they have caramelised.

Blend the caramel apples in a food processor until they are smooth.

Gently fold the whipped cream into the caramel apple mixture.

ORANGE AND ALMOND CAKE

Preparation time: 25 minutes
Total cooking time: 3 hours
Serves 6–8

2 large navel oranges
6 eggs, separated
1 tablespoon orange blossom water or orange liqueur
1 cup (250 g) caster sugar
300 g ground almonds
1 teaspoon baking powder
3 navel oranges, to garnish
cream, to serve (optional)

Orange syrup
2 cups (500 ml) fresh orange juice, strained
3/4 cup (185 g) caster sugar
1/4 cup (60 ml) Sauternes

1 Grease and lightly flour a 23 cm springform cake tin, tipping out any excess flour.
2 Wipe the oranges with a damp cloth to remove any dirt. Place the whole oranges into a medium saucepan full of water and boil for 2 hours, topping up with water as it evaporates. Remove the oranges.
3 Preheat the oven to moderate 180°C (350°F/Gas 4). Cut the oranges into quarters and place in a food processor. Process until smooth, then cool thoroughly.
4 Place the egg yolks, orange blossom water and caster sugar in a large bowl and beat until smooth, then stir in the orange purée and mix well. Whisk the egg whites in a clean, dry bowl until firm peaks form.
5 Add the ground almonds and baking powder to the orange mixture, stir together well, then carefully fold in the egg whites. Gently pour into the prepared cake tin and place on the middle shelf of the oven for 1 hour, or until firm to touch. Cover the cake with foil if it is browning too quickly. Cool the cake in the tin before transferring it to a serving plate.
6 Meanwhile, to make the syrup, place the orange juice, sugar and Sauternes in a saucepan over medium heat and stir until the sugar is dissolved. Reduce the heat and simmer for about 20 minutes, or until reduced by half and slightly syrupy, skimming off any scum that forms on the surface. The syrup will thicken as it cools.
7 Peel the extra oranges and remove all pith and sinew. Cut each orange into thin slices. Cut the cake into wedges and top with orange slices and drizzle with the syrup. Delicious served with cream.

NUTRITION PER SERVE (8)
Protein 13 g; Fat 25 g; Carbohydrate 70 g; Dietary Fibre 4.5 g; Cholesterol 135 mg; 2247kJ (537 cal)

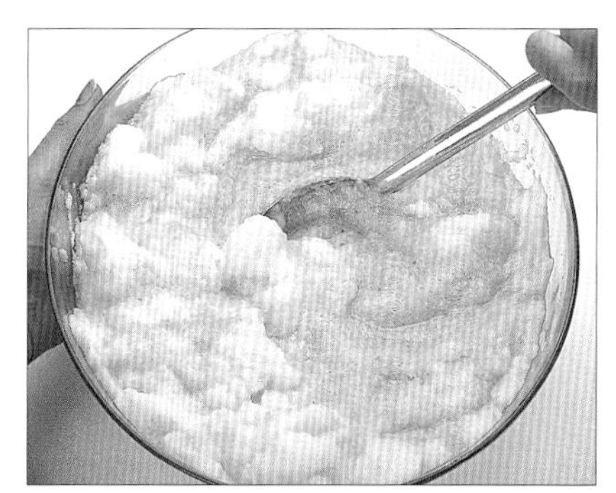

Carefully fold the egg whites into the orange mixture.

Simmer the orange syrup until reduced by half.

Peel the oranges, removing all the pith, then cut into thin slices.

CHOCOLATE CROISSANT PUDDING

Preparation time: 10 minutes + 10 minutes cooling
Total cooking time: 50 minutes
Serves 6–8

4 croissants, torn into pieces
100 g dark chocolate, chopped into pieces
4 eggs
1/3 cup (90 g) caster sugar
1 cup (250 ml) milk
1 cup (250 ml) cream
1/2 teaspoon grated orange rind
1/3 cup (80 ml) orange juice
2 tablespoons coarsely chopped hazelnuts

1 Preheat the oven to moderate 180°C (350°F/Gas 4). Grease the base and side of a 20 cm deep-sided cake tin and line the bottom of the tin with baking paper.
2 Place the croissant pieces in the tin, then scatter evenly with chocolate.
3 Beat the eggs and sugar together until pale and creamy.
4 Heat the milk and cream in a saucepan to almost boiling, then remove from the heat. Gradually pour into the egg mixture, stirring constantly. Add the orange rind and juice and stir well.
5 Slowly pour the mixture over the croissants, allowing the liquid to be absorbed before adding more. Sprinkle the top with the hazelnuts and bake for 45 minutes, or until a skewer comes out clean when inserted in the centre.
6 Cool for 10 minutes. Run a knife around the edge, then turn out and invert. Cut into wedges and serve warm with cream, if desired.

NUTRITION PER SERVE (8)
Protein 6.5 g; Fat 24 g; Carbohydrate 24 g; Dietary Fibre 0.5 g; Cholesterol 137 mg; 1382 kJ (330 cal)

Scatter the chocolate pieces evenly over the croissants.

Beat the eggs and sugar together until pale and creamy.

Slowly pour the creamy mixture over the croissants.

INDEX

INTERNATIONAL GLOSSARY OF INGREDIENTS

capsicum	red or green pepper	fresh coriander	fresh cilantro
eggplant	aubergine	tomato purée (Aus.)	sieved crushed tomatoes/ passata (UK)
tomato paste (Aus.)	tomato purée, double concentrate (UK)	zucchini	courgette

Published by Murdoch Books®, a division of Murdoch Magazines Pty Limited,
GPO Box 1203, Sydney NSW 1045.

Managing Editor: Rachel Carter **Editor:** Zoë Harpham **Designer:** Michelle Cutler **Food Director:** Jody Vassallo **Managing Food Editor:** Jane Lawson **Recipe Development:** Ruth Armstrong, Fiona Hammond, Eva Katz, Jane Lawson, Michelle Lawton, Barbara Lowery, Kerrie Mullins, Kate Murdoch, Maria Papadopoulos, Wendy Quisumbing, Jody Vassallo **Home Economists:** Valli Little, Ben Masters, Briget Palmer, Wendy Quisumbing **Nutritionist:** Thérèse Abbey **Photographers:** Ian Hofstetter, Reg Morrison (steps) **Food Stylist:** Michelle Noerianto **Food Preparation:** Valli Little, Justine Johnson, Kate Murdoch **UK Consultant:** Maggi Altham **CEO & Publisher:** Anne Wilson.
The nutritional information provided for each recipe does not include garnishes or accompaniments, such as rice, unless they are included in specific quantities in the ingredients. The values are approximations and can be affected by biological and seasonal variations in food, the unknown composition of some manufactured foods and uncertainty in the dietary database. Nutrient data given are derived primarily from the NUTTAB95 database produced by the Australian New Zealand Food Authority.

National Library of Australia Cataloguing-in-Publication Data. Modern Australian food. Includes index. ISBN 0 86411 956 9. 1. Cookery, Australian. I. Title: Family circle (Sydney, N.S.W.). (Series: Family circle step-by-step). 641.5994. First printed 2000. Printed by Prestige Litho, Queensland. PRINTED IN AUSTRALIA. Australian distribution to supermarkets and newsagents by Gordon and Gotch Ltd, 68 Kingsgrove Road, Belmore, NSW 2182. Distributed in NZ by Golden Press, a division of HarperCollins Publishers, 31 View Road, Glenfield, PO Box 1, Auckland 1.